CONTAINER GARDENING

CONTAINER GARDENING

HAZEL EVANS

OCTOPUS
BOOKS

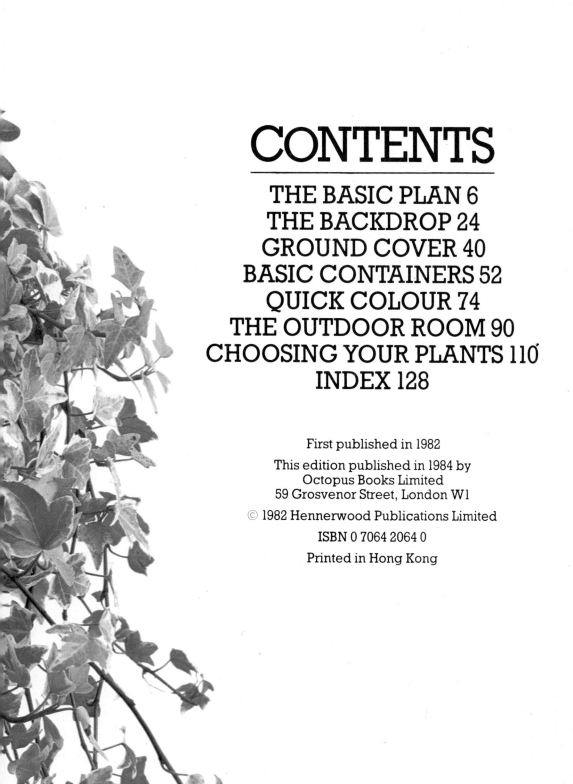

CONTENTS

First published in 1982

This edition published in 1984 by
Octopus Books Limited
59 Grosvenor Street, London W1

© 1982 Hennerwood Publications Limited

ISBN 0 7064 2064 0

Printed in Hong Kong

THE BASIC PLAN

It is amazing how much garden you can conjure up in the space of just a few square metres if you use instant aids like tubs and boxes to do so. With container-grown plants now on sale everywhere, it takes only a short time to provide colour wherever you want it out of doors, and something green to look at all the year round. And if all you have is a window-sill to work on, do not lose heart. With climbers around the frame, trailers in front and some flowering evergreens for all-year-round interest, you can have an ever-changing scene of interest.

A balcony gives you much more scope – somewhere to sit; somewhere to grow permanent trees in tubs; with perennials to give you flowers year after year. Bright bedding plants can be used to change the mood when spring comes along. By providing shelter you can often grow half hardy plants that would normally die off in the winter. And by the clever use of two mirrors, one on each side, you can appear to have an outdoor room that stretches to infinity. Even grass is no problem – you can buy fake turf that can be rolled up and taken indoors when it rains, but provides a brilliant emerald-green sward on which to put a deckchair, a foil for those summer annuals planted around the sides.

With a flat roof to play with, you have a potential perfumed paradise in the sky, which can be anything from a formal Elizabethan knot-garden to a tropical jungle,

with creepers running riot over the rooftops. Unconventional and unpromising spots like basement areas, too, can provide an unexpected mini-garden with a fountain and ferns, spotlighted at night to turn it into an emerald-green bower.

Given a few tubs and troughs, even the meanest back yard can burst into bloom. The smallest place can house a rockery, a pool, or even a waterfall. If time is at a premium, then paving can be used to create a garden that calls for very little work. Planted with herbs and alpines in the crevices and cracks, it becomes a delightful place in which to relax. And labour-saving ideas, such as the use of ground-cover plants, will make the work of tending surrounding flower beds easier too. Privacy can be achieved for a few pounds, with trellis decked out in flowering climbers.

All such places are a challenge; the more unpromising the plot you are faced with, the more you are spurred on to fill it with a 'technicolour' display. It becomes a point of honour to see just how much you can cram into a window-box or a tub, to work out ways to blot out a concrete wilderness with a screen of living plants.

Instant gardening – container gardening – becomes a way of life. You are constantly thinking up new ways to beat the system and surround yourself with colour and greenery against the odds. You can garden in almost anything if you try – tanks, bottles,

Page 6 The harsh outlines of brick and concrete in this city garden have been softened by blocks and containers of green plants. Note how the change in level provides added interest and more growing space.

Right An ingenious way of using a very small space: a miscellany of jars and bottles that not only make unusual plant containers but lend their own colours to the scene.

Opposite page A tropical touch on an elegant town balcony. The twin yuccas give an exotic look to match the architecture.

discarded plastic cartons, anything that comes to hand. You can choose between two-colour chic or a riot of different shades of flowers, all for the price of a seed packet. What is more, you can shift the colour around to precisely where you want it, changing your mind at the slightest whim.

Surveying your site

First of all, work out what you are going to do with your small area – have an overall plan. For however tiny the space available, it should have a recognizable purpose.

Is there room to sit in it? And, if so, do you want to sit in it? It could be that you are overlooked, or that the garden is in shade all the time, or that the street is so noisy that you are not likely to want to stay outside. In this case you can fill the area with plants and leave standing room only. If you have a balcony on which you want to sit, you may have to sacrifice some of the planting space to make room for a deckchair; again, that is something to be decided at this stage.

Has the area got to work for its living? Do you have to store dustbins in it, or hang out the washing? It may be necessary to find space to keep a bicycle, scooter, or pushchair under cover. Make a note of any such items that have to be taken into consideration.

Work out which way your plot faces and which way the sun shines, and how it affects your mode of life. You may find, for instance, when you come to chart the sunshine, that the spot where you are planning to sunbathe in the afternoon, in a small back yard or on a balcony, will be in the shade at that time of day; in which case you will have to think again. It is important, too, to note which parts of the area get the most sun. Some plants will obligingly put up with all sorts of conditions, including shade. But others must have direct sunlight in order to survive. Remember that in summer the sun climbs higher in the sky and you get longer hours of heat and light.

Screening off the neighbours and ensuring privacy, too, has to be done in such a way that it does not put the garden into shade or make it feel cramped. This can often be done by using a see-through structure such as trellis or pierced-screen concrete blocks, rather than a solid wall. But remember that the higher the fence, the less sunshine it will let in, and that pierced screening of some sort is often better for climbing plants. It allows the air to circulate around them, and avoids down-draughts.

If your plot already has a tree growing in it, then you must allow for the shade that it creates, and remember that only certain

This very small space, which is scarcely more than a sitting-out area, has been crammed with a rich variety of plants that not only make an interesting view from the window but help to screen off noise from neighbours.

plants will grow under it – white clover (*Trifolium repens*), for instance, which acts as ground cover and does not mind poor soil and shade. The same goes for an existing hedge, which will leech out all the nutrients from the soil for a foot or so in front of it, making it difficult to grow anything there. Other factors must also be considered: are you dominated by a high-rise building which shuts out a lot of light? And is yours a site that gets more than its fair share of wind? In the case of roof gardens or high-sited balconies this is almost certainly bound to be the case.

Note any existing features that are there, and plan to make the most of them. Even a dead woody shrub or tree is useful for a climber such as a clematis to scramble over, so do not be in too much of a hurry to root it out unless it really is in the way.

How is your garden going to be viewed? Balconies and window boxes will, inevitably, be framed by a window or French doors. Then there is the street-side view of them to consider as well. If it is a backyard, you will want to look at it as well

as sit in it – but from what angle? It could be, for instance, particularly if the garden is linked to the basement, that you will view it mainly from above.

Make a note of the good and bad points of the area you are going to work with: you will need to take them all into account. And if you are taking over after the builders have been in, do not be in too much of a hurry to throw everything out until you have decided what to do out of doors. Old windows make good, cheap cold frames for raising plants, for instance. Rubble may be useful as foundation hardcore for a path or a terrace. And off-cuts of timber can come in handy for made-to-measure window-boxes or for sawing into shelves.

Before making ambitious plans for a roof garden or a terrace, check that the existing structure is strong enough to take laden containers. These are surprisingly heavy when filled with plants and damp soil. If there is a problem, it may be possible to get round it by using light pots with peat or vermiculite composts, which are lighter than conventional soil. If you are in any doubt, it

Opposite page Make the most of any unusual existing features in your garden. Here an old tree stump has been used to provide a setting for vivid annuals.

Below High-sited balconies and roof gardens need to offer at least some protection from winds if the plants are to thrive. In this roof garden slatted-wood screening and an overhead trellis give welcome shelter to climbers such as clematis.

is a good idea to get an expert in. And if you are doing anything drastic you need to check that you are not contravening local bye-laws or a landlord's agreement. It is far better to find out beforehand than to have to put things right afterwards – expensively. Remember that many trees now have preservation orders on them, especially in towns; this is a point that needs checking too.

It is useful, at this stage, to find out what type of soil you have – acid, alkaline (limy), or neutral. And find out whether it is a sticky clay or a lightweight sand that will let the moisture drain through. If you are gardening solely in containers then you can choose your own compost to suit yourself. Otherwise, a chat with the neighbours or the use of a soil testing kit will give you a guideline when it comes to choosing plants. If you have no-one else to turn to, your local town parks department may be of help.

Acid-loving plants, such as rhododendrons, camellias, and some of the heathers, will not tolerate an alkaline soil, such as chalk or limestone (they show it quickly with yellowed leaves), so you must grow them in special soil in pots or raised beds. Clematis, on the other hand, loves soil with lime in it and will thrive in these conditions.

Planning the site

A great deal of time and money can be saved if you draw up a plan of your site, even if it is nothing much more than a largish balcony. The plan gives you a chance to make your mistakes on paper rather than more expensively on the site. The easiest way to do this is to make a large-scale plan of your plot on graph paper. Using the squares to count, rather than measuring each time, saves a great deal of effort. And you can sketch in the approximate size of fully grown specimen plants to see how they will look. Better still, cut them out of pieces of paper and move them around on your plan to find the best position for them. If you are proposing to include deckchairs, cushions, or a table and chairs, cut out scale outlines of the furniture separately and move them around on your plan to see if they fit. You will need to make sure that it is actually possible to pull a chair back from the table and stand up, especially if you are building a terrace in a confined space or cramming a number of containers around seating on a balcony.

Have a good look at the building that starts your plot. Sometimes there is a built-in ladder, or a fire escape, or a drain pipe that you have scarcely noticed before, but that

will put paid to any idea of having a box against that wall. On a roof garden a TV aerial may intrude. Bear in mind, too, if you are planning raised flower beds or putting plants against a house wall where there as never been a bed before, that you must make sure you do not go above the damp-course line, or you will be plagued with moisture on the inside of the house. You can find this vital line if you look for a layer of tarred felt or other material inserted between the bricks near the ground on newer houses or, perhaps, a series of holes bored in the wall on older properties. Where no damp course is evident, follow the general guide that the soil level should be a good 150 mm (6 in) below the floor level inside the house.

If you do come up against the problem of damp, then you must either move the flower bed away from the wall, put your plants in freestanding containers, or put some sort of permanent waterproof sheeting between the soil and the brickwork. Another simple idea is to use growing bags, which contain the soil in plastic. You can disguise them in some way – with a row of pot-grown herbs, for instance.

The next step, having laid your garden out on paper to your satisfaction, is to try it out on the site. On a balcony use pieces of wood, buckets and any other props available to section off the area where you are planning to put your boxes and tubs – drawers make good substitute boxes for this. You may find that what you have planned takes up too much room and that what seemed to work on paper does not quite work out in practice. Perhaps the door or window will not open, for instance, because something is in the way.

The same goes when planning a roof garden or a small yard. Mark out paved areas, flower beds, and so on with a string and wooden pegs. Keep the string above ground level to give a more realistic feel of that third dimension – height; a planned area marked with chalk on the ground may seem feasible that way, but obtrusive when you see it in terms of growing plants. If your plot slopes, do not be in too much of a hurry to level it up. Think carefully first. It might be better to turn it into a series of terraces. Or the slope could be turned into a feature with an attractive trickle of water down to a pool – you can now buy prefabricated waterfall and stream kits from water-garden specialists. Remember that the more levels of planting you can achieve, the more space you are making to grow flowers. The same goes on a balcony, where stepped window-boxes will give you more colour, and extra

Even a cramped, concrete basement area like this can be nicely brightened up. Pot plants perched on the side of the steps make a colourful view from the window.

boxes fixed securely outside the rail as well as inside will give you a considerable amount of extra growing space.

Decide, too, whether you want to block out your surroundings or make a feature of them. Often an item like a church spire or a magnificent tree across the road can make a punctuation point outside your garden that you want to keep in view, while an ugly factory or lines of neighbours' washing will need screening from sight.

Giving your garden a 'look'

You can have fun in a small space by choosing a theme for your plot. The 'Mediterranean look' makes a good choice if you have a space that you use mainly as an outdoor room. This could be dominated by flowers, with the hardy *Hibiscus syriacus* mixed with cool camellias and geraniums that are allowed to sprawl. And, as a substitute for the cypresses that show up like exclamation marks in a Mediterranean landscape, you could plant Lawson's cypress (*Chamaecyparis lawsoniana* 'Columnaris'), which will grow in a small bed or a tub.

The 'tropical look' works well on a formal terrace. This can include *Yucca gloriosa* with its short trunk and needle-like leaves, and the Chusan palm (*Trachycarpus fortunei*) if you have a little more space. These could be joined by some of your indoor plants, the rubber plant (*Ficus elastica*) or the Swiss-cheese plant (*Monstera deliciosa*), for instance, in mid-summer.

A dramatic way to treat an area that is little more than a back yard is to turn it into a miniature jungle – this is a good treatment for a corner, too. You could have a background of bamboo and pampas grass with a creeper – the Russian vine (*Polygonum baldschuanicum*) would be splendid here – to entangle itself around them. In the foreground, put some of the large ornamental forms of rhubarb – *Rheum palmatum*, for instance, with its huge purple-red leaves, or the South American prickly rhubarb (*Gunnera manicata*), which needs a damp soil but could take the place of a tree. Then you could underplant with hostas, which would enjoy the shade of the other taller plants, and, here again, during the summer months your rubber plant and Swiss-cheese plant would look good. Taking the jungle look further, the false castor-oil plant (*Fatsia japonica*) will survive out of doors in a sheltered place all year round, and you can even try the true fruiting banana (*Musa paradisiaca*) if you put some

A strong, simple theme can work particularly well in a confined space. Here the basement area of a town house has been given a Japanese look. The bamboo growing in the foreground is echoed by bamboo trellis and slatting against the wall and the whole scheme is drawn together by the large ornamental piece.

sacking or straw over it in the winter months (it may seem to be killed off by heavy frosts, but it will usually throw up fresh suckers in the spring).

Another idea for a small space, such as a roof garden or possibly even a balcony, is to take the traditional willow-pattern plate and bring it to life, either in miniature on a window-sill, using bonsai trees and a sink garden, or on a somewhat larger scale in a courtyard using dwarf trees. Water is essential for this, but you could have a small stream using an underwater pump. Pebbles can be found on the beach or on sale in builders' yards, and for a very small scale stream you can use gravel, obtainable from aquarium shops.

An 'English country garden look' is the direct opposite of the formalized oriental style of planting. In this case you need to hide the boundaries of your plot as much as possible with greenery, so that it appears to go on indefinitely. Although apparently unplanned, this type of plot needs careful design if it is to work in a small space. Ivy-covered walls help to establish the backdrop if you are dealing with nothing much more than a basement area. And it is better to have not a formal path but stepping stones set in a 'grass' of green chamomile (*Anthemis nobilis*). The cottage-garden look lends itself well to small areas, even a balcony, where foxgloves and hollyhocks will thrive and will delight passers-by. You should start if possible by planting at least two climbers, such as honeysuckle (*Lonicera*) with a clematis or one of the old climbing roses, to set the scene. Then cram in a multicoloured patchwork spread of flowers, such as red-hot poker (*Kniphofia*), golden rod (*Solidago*), and Michaelmas daisies (*Aster novi-belgii*), with a border of pinks (*Dianthus*) or thrift (*Armeria*). Remember that with many cottage-garden flowers, the perennials tend to take over, so you will have to prune them out ruthlessly in the autumn. The planting should be apparently haphazard (though it makes good sense to put the tallest plants at the back), but the edge of the bed should be straight and formalized, for your primary intention here is to reproduce a flower border in miniature.

Do not forget the old-fashioned country flowers like lamb's ears (*Stachys lanata*), which has purple flowers and furry grey leaves, Solomon's seal (*Polygonatum multiflorum*), and bleeding heart (*Dicentra*). And you must have one of the compact versions of lavender (*Lavandula spica*) – 'Hidcote Blue' is a good one to look out for. More cottage-garden flowers that grow well

in tubs, small beds, and window boxes include the everlasting flower (*Helichrysum*), honesty (*Lunaria*), which has distinctive silvery seed pods, and sea lavender (*Limonium*). The flowers of all these will dry successfully and give you indoor memories of summer all the winter, making even more use of a small space.

A fuss-free, all-year-round display can be planned, carefully, for window boxes or small gardens using nothing but bulbs, corms, and rhizomes, starting in the beginning of the year with snowdrops (*Galanthus*) and crocuses (*Crocus*). In early spring come daffodils (*Narcissus*) and tulips (*Tulipa*), then bluebells (*Endymion*

nonscriptus) and fritillaries (*Fritillaria*). In early summer, lily-of-the-valley (*Convallaria majalis*) appears. Next come the taller plants like *Montbretia*, which is more delicate than its relative, *Gladiolus*, and nerines, those striking pink lilies from South Africa. Then in autumn it is time for autumn crocuses (*Colchicum autumnale*) and autumn snowdrops (*Galanthus nivalis reginae-olgae*), ending up with winter aconites (*Eranthis hyemalis*) at the turn of the year.

One-colour gardens look good in a small space – all white, all gold (homing in on plants like golden privet, *Ligustrum ovalifolium*, grown in a tub and clipped into shape), or one of silver-blue, using silver-leaved plants and miniature blue-toned conifers.

A small formal backyard can be turned, very easily, into a formal herb garden by the careful choice of plant containers. Rectangular boxes placed to form the outline of a series of squares, for instance, each inside the other, surrounding a large round tub in the middle. In this way a surprisingly large number of herbs can be planted in a relatively small space, and the effect is very striking, especially if the centrepiece is a mop-headed standard bay tree (*Laurus nobilis*).

Finally, for a really dramatic effect, you

A water tank can make a modest but attractive free-standing pool for a patio, terrace, or roof garden. Water-lilies and other aquatics will thrive in a setting like this.

19

could turn a whole balcony or a backyard into a water garden with water lilies (to provide the colour), bog-loving plants, fountains, and fish. Even a plastic window-box without any drainage holes could become a small water garden in itself, filled with miniature lilies. While you are making long-term planting plans, work on some instant window-dressing of colour to keep you going. In the case of window-boxes this might well be a mass of bedding plants picked up cheaply in the local market, while you ponder over other things – dwarf conifers, for instance, – that will form the basis of your permanent mini-garden.

Other effects

Think of your plot as another room in your apartment or house, and treat it as such. Above all, do not forget the walls. In a window-box set-up, the side ledges outside the windows can be used for climbers, provided there is still space for the windows to open. Even casement windows do not preclude some colour – window-boxes can be fixed on brackets underneath the sill or used *inside* instead.

Fences and walls are a precious bonus to the confined gardener, and they are the places where you can get some of your most spectacular effects by using unconventional items like mirrors to deceive the eye.

Consider the 'floor'. What is it going to be used for? Heavy-duty traffic may dictate the use of concrete or paving stones, but they can be jazzed up by growing little crevice plants between them. Remember, though, that the use of paving under a deciduous tree or a bush that bears lots of berries may mean that you will have a great deal of sweeping up to do when autumn comes if it is not to look unsightly, and it may pay you to have grass or a grass substitute instead.

If a patch of lawn is out of the question, but you yearn for one, then you can have a miniature patch of green chamomile or some other creeping plant that makes a good grass substitute. On a balcony you can even have your own 'portable lawn' if you plant a shallow square tray with a creeping matting green plant.

Even the smallest spot needs a focal point of some sort, something to feast your eye on when you view it. A statue, if it is carefully chosen, can lead the eye to the end of a small courtyard. A sundial makes a good centre point to a paved garden. A pool looks good, especially if it is raised above ground level for dramatic effect. On a balcony it is more likely to be something on a smaller

A delightful example of a town garden exploiting its two levels to the best advantage: the pool, which appears as a raised point of interest on one level, is viewed from above on the upper, sitting-out level.

scale; a particularly attractively shaped dwarf evergreen, for instance, or a tiny fountain. In a really small, dull area, you could use bonsai trees in pots placed on shelves bracketed to the wall.

By night you can play all sorts of tricks with the aid of outdoor lighting. A small floodlit garden can look very dramatic indeed, even if it is still at the weed-covered stage. And spotlights can be placed strategically at ground level to light up one particular feature – a statue or a clump of flowers or foliage, for instance, and moved around as the seasons change. Having your backyard or balcony floodlit on a summer night will make your living space seem much larger and give a new dimension to your house or apartment rooms.

Learn to make the most of what space you have, and grow some good things to eat. Cordon fruit trees in pots, for instance, make a good side edging for a balcony. And you can grow an amazing number of salad vegetables in tubs and boxes. Strawberries, too, make marvellous ground cover in a small space, even if you can spare room only for the small alpine variety, 'Baron Solemacher'. When you come to plant your plot for the first time, do keep a plan of what has gone where, however small the pot. It is all too easy to sow seeds in containers around growing shrubs or put small seedlings in a raised bed and then forget about their existence and absent-mindedly weed them out a week or so later. It is a good idea to invest in a set of garden labels and an indelible pencil (you can get them at most garden shops and centres) so that precious or unusual plants can have their own markers. But hang on to your planting plan as well, as seedlings may be knocked out of the ground by marauding cats.

Trees are precious in a city plot, so do plan to invest in one – and more than one if you can find the space for them. There are many small trees that can survive in crowded conditions – flowering cherries (*Prunus*), for instance, and miniature weeping willows such as *Salix repens*. There is also the miniature silver birch (*Betula nana*), which will not make more than 1.5 m (5 ft) of growth and goes a coppery-red shade in the autumn. Even a window-sill can have its own miniature weeping willow – *Salix helvetica* will not grow more than 900 mm (3 ft) high, and can be kept in a pot.

Mini-greenhouses

The judicious use of glass and plastic can work wonders in a small area to bring on plants, to start off seedlings, and to cheat the weather. It will also extend the flowering season of delicate specimen plants. Consider buying a mini-greenhouse to raise pot plants and early salad vegetables too. There is one, for instance, made from PVC stretched over a framework, that is 1.5 m (5 ft) high and just over 1.2 m (4 ft) long by 600 mm (2 ft) deep. It fits easily onto a balcony. In this you can raise an amazing number of seeds and go on to grow tomatoes, cucumbers, and peppers. It has trays, too, with capillary matting to cut down on the chore of watering. When you have finished using it, you can dismantle it and pack it away neatly into a cupboard. Or you can add lighting and heating apparatus and use it through the winter to raise out-of-season salads, or do something more exotic – propagating African violets (*Saintpaulia*), for instance. There are other, rather more substantial mini-greenhouses made from glass that are fixed, lean-to style, like glass cupboards against a house wall and these, too, will fit onto a balcony.

temporary glasshouses. Empty jam jars or glass tumblers can be popped over strawberries to protect them from birds and help them to ripen, and will lie on their sides in a window-box almost unnoticed. They can also be used to bring on plants such as crocuses during the winter months. An early window-box or hanging basket can be helped along in a cold spring if a cloche or a tunnel of plastic is fixed over it. You can use it to warm up the soil, this way, before sowing seeds, too. And if all you have is a window-sill to grow on, you can still have your greenhouse: just stretch some tough clear PVC over it, indoors or out, like double glazing, put the plants inside, and see them thrive. It is best to nail the plastic at the top, or fix it to a wooden batten and screw that in place, then weight the bottom in some way – a batten of heavy hardwood along the bottom edge is good for this purpose, as you will want to lift the plastic frequently to attend to your plants.

Things around the house can be used as mini-greenhouses too. An oven-glass bowl, for instance, can be used as a temporary growing dome over a bowl or tub of plants. If you are taking cuttings, clear plastic sandwich bags come in handy – make a wire hoop and put it like a handle into each pot, then upend the bag over it and secure it round the pot with an elastic band. Provided the plant was properly watered in the first place, and its leaves are not allowed to touch the plastic (when the effect of sunlight would be to scorch them), it should stay happily like that for some time without needing to be watered.

A cleverly planned window-box in which the trailing plants lead the eye down to the plantings below. Twin miniature conifers, which make a permanent feature of the box, are echoed by larger conifers on the level below. Careful grouping of bedding plants gives scope for colourful variation from season to season.

THE BACKDROP

You can almost double the potential growing space of your balcony, patio, or garden if you use the boundary walls in an imaginative way. Climbers on the walls of a house, for instance, can turn them into part of the garden scheme and bring flowers close to the windows. Climbers can also be used to hide unsightly items like sheds, or to screen off a view that you would rather not see. The opportunities are endless.

A climber can frame a window. Morning glory (*Ipomoea*), grown in pots, for instance, can be trained up lines of twine around the window. Or you can build a narrow trellis and grow climbers up that. Even a humble chain-link fence can have a climber, such as common ivy (*Hedera helix*), trained and tied to it so that it is completely covered and becomes a lush green 'wall'. And you can even make yourself a portable screen of green for a window-box: build a wooden plant trough with two vertical pieces of wood attached at either end, then stretch wires across to support climbing plants.

Walls, fences, and screens

The smaller the plot you are dealing with, the more important the boundary walls become. They are of overwhelming importance in a place such as a basement 'area', for instance, because you just cannot avoid them and they are probably blocking out not just a view but also a great deal of light. However, a lot can be done to improve matters – white paint on wood or brickwork brightens up the area and makes it seem more spacious, as well as reflecting more light into your rooms. It is particularly effective in narrow passageways of the kind that are often found alongside terrace houses. Here two white walls are better than one, for they reflect the available light onto each other and double its effect.

A walled garden in a town may be more shaded than an open country garden, but it does have the advantage that it gives shelter, creating a micro-climate of warmth for the plants inside. This is why it is often possible to grow plants that are considered half-hardy in a town garden. In the same way, screens with climbers on them on the side of a balcony or around a roof garden will make it warmer and more sheltered. Remember that climbers and trailers can be planted in boxes on top of a wall so as to hang down. And while your climbers are growing you can paint fake flowers on the wall – make a simple stencil and use artists' acrylic colours for the job.

If you are starting from scratch, there is a wide variety of fencing to choose from.

Right A fantasy garden in a small space. The giant colour picture provides a backdrop for bold plantings of bedding colour and some amusing pieces of statuary. The whole scene is framed by a splendid *Clematis jackmanii*.

Page 24 A colourful way to cover a wall, *Abutilon vitifolium*, here cascading over a trellis, will grow well in any sheltered spot.

Brick walls are beautiful, but they are expensive to build. If you have inherited some, then you are lucky, for they store heat and anything that grows against them will prosper. Pierced-concrete screen blocks make a see-through wall that can be very attractive – screening off part of a terrace, for instance – and they have the advantage of letting plenty of air circulate around plants that grow against them. If you have solid walls and the yard seems airless and damp, consider putting in pierced blocks or airbricks in the wall dividing two gardens, if your neighbour will agree. This helps to dry the area out, and is healthier for the plants. Wattle fencing gives a country look in town surroundings, but can look rather untidy. Woven lap fencing is relatively easy to put up, as it comes in large panels and is easy to locate. If you have inherited a chain-link fence, then you may feel you want to grow some tall screening plants to give it a more permanent feeling. Do not despise openwork fences; they make good frames for climbing plants and let in light and air.

Arches and pergolas can be used in even the most minute garden to give height and interest and to act as hosts for climbing plants. In a small area an arch is a particularly good way of shutting out an unwanted view, such as a high-rise block, as it acts as a kind of roof – indeed, if you want to, you can lay heavy plastic sheeting over the top to cover it in and keep out some of the weather. Other ways to achieve height in a small space include making a 'wigwam' of bamboo or rustic poles and growing climbers up that. Make sure that you poke the poles well into the ground before you plant, otherwise the weight of the climber, especially if it tends to pull to one side, may cause them to topple. The same sort of idea can be used on a balcony in a large tub to give that much-needed extra dimension of height. Trellis put a few inches in front of a wall with climbers trained up it gives a feeling of extra depth.

Using screening on a roof garden needs extra care. You are bound to get high winds from time to time and this could topple anything that is not very securely fixed. You will need screens for both shade and shelter or fragile plants will tend to bake in hot sun and break in high winds. Remember, too, if you are putting climbers on a roof that they prefer their roots to be shaded in some way – if you have an underplanting of herbaceous plants then this will happen naturally.

On a balcony you can get added privacy and shelter by using side screens. You could consider using lengths of canvas sailcloth the way yachtsmen use it for the sides of boat cockpits as a cheap and easy way to achieve this effect. Three identically high walls are not necessarily the best idea. They can give a boxed in appearance and it often pays to have one higher or lower than the other two.

If you are faced with a solid, smooth wall, then you will probably want to put plenty of things on it. To save banging in dozens of nails and vine-eyes, it might pay you to cover it with fine netting to let plants scramble over it. If, for some reason or other, you cannot bang nails into the wall (perhaps the place you are living in is rented or the wall belongs to a neighbour) then you can erect a trellis an inch or so in front of it; use the squared-off kind which is more rigid than the diamond-shaped

Opposite page This exotic, specially constructed trelliswork lets the air through, but keeps draughts out of a small basement garden, while also offering a measure of privacy. A similar scheme could be constructed using laths.

Below Giant swags of container-grown ivy cascade down the front of this town house. Trained on ropes suspended from the penthouse at the top, they can be pulled away from the front of the building when the latter needs to be repainted.

variety. Trellis can now be bought in plastic. This is more expensive than wooden trellis but it requires no maintenance. In between trellis and netting come all sorts of rigid plastic-coated wire meshes – look at the small advertisements in Sunday papers and gardening magazines, and go to garden centres to see what is on offer. Mesh or netting can often be used to increase growing space on a balcony, if you can get permission to stretch it and fix the top to the base of the balcony above. Or it can be stretched like canvas on a wooden frame for clematis and other lightweight climbers to use. A zigzag of trellis on a fence can increase the growing space involved. Use the side that faces the house for decorative climbers and the side away from the house for runner beans, peas and tomatoes. The sharper the angle of the trellis the more wall space you create. Or you could use an openwork frame of bamboo, set at right angles to the wall with decorative plants on one side and vegetables on the other.

Plants for walls

If you have a wall, or an unsightly building that you want to cover rapidly, then the fastest, most vigorous climber you are likely to come across is Russian vine (*Polygonum baldschuanicum*), which can cover 6 m (20 ft) of wall in the space of one season. However, the trouble is that once having started it, it is difficult to get it to stop. It is deciduous, too, so you are left with bare branches in winter. But judiciously clipped and pruned back, it quite quickly forms a thick network of trunks which makes it an attractive proposition for, say, a pergola where you want leaves overhead, and its long delicate racemes of white flowers hang down in an attractive way. It is a good choice to compensate for a slower growing, more attractive climber like a vine or wisteria provided you keep it under control. Two other rapid climbers to look for are *Clematis montana* varieties and *Rosa filipes* 'Kiftsgate', a very vigorous rambler with white flowers that will eventually need checking. Clematis can also be used to scramble over an existing bush or tree. More instant cover is provided by the perennial climbing nasturtium, Scottish flame (*Tropaeolum speciosum*), which grows fast while permanent climbers are becoming established.

Tall plants to consider putting against a wall to brighten it up on a temporary basis include sunflowers (*Helianthus annuus*), tall delphiniums, foxgloves (*Digitalis purpurea*), hollyhocks (*Althaea rosea*), and

black-eyed susan (*Rudbeckia hirta*). Outdoor tomatoes will climb to a reasonable height if you pinch out their side shoots; so will cucumbers.

As another short-term proposition, runner beans make decorative quick climbers that gives you a crop to eat as well. The blue cocoa bean is attractive too. Fruits such as loganberries, gooseberries, and raspberries can be grown in a single row or in tubs to give colour and fruits, and fruit trees can be trained against walls as cordons. You can even grow cordon fruit trees in tubs and train them to run along the side of a balcony and eventually make a mini-fence.

Then there are a number of free-standing shrubs that will grow anything up to 2.5 m (8 ft) high and can be used in place of climbers where the backdrop is not able to take them – chain link fencing for instance. The best known of these is the Leyland cypress (× *Cupressocyparis leylandii*), which makes a quick-growing hedge. If you want a different effect, plant them in pairs and tie their tops together so that they bend to form a series of arches. If you have the space for it there is the astonishing ten-foot-a-year grass (*Miscanthus sacchariflorus*), an ornamental grass that makes a marvellous windbreak, though it dies down each winter to leave a screen of stalks.

Several of the free-standing shrubs that can be grown against a wall have attractive berries in the autumn. *Berberis darwinii*, for instance, follows its bright yellow flowers in spring with dark purple berries, while species of *Cotoneaster*, which bear white or pink flowers in June, have rich red berries that stay on for most of the winter. The various firethorns (*Pyracantha*) have masses of red, orange, or yellow berries and are also good for free-standing hedges.

A country setting is attractive. In town gardens in particular, to have the sides of a garden clothed in green gives it much more of a country look. The first and most obvious choice for this is the trio of climbers that have been used in the country as a matter of habit for years; there are few old cottages that do not have their rambling rose, clematis or honeysuckle over the door, and using this trio, you can very successfully get a country look in town.

Some climbers are self supporting and do not need help in the form of netting or wires – common ivy (*Hedera helix*), for instance, Boston ivy (*Parthenocissus tricuspidata* 'Veitchii') and Virginia creeper (*P. quinquefolia*). Choose a variegated form of *H. helix*, such as 'Chicago', or one with golden leaves; this will give you a very

Chimney pots can sometimes be picked up very cheaply in demolition yards, and they convert into splendid plinths or containers for instant plantings. Here such a container is backed by an attractive climbing rose.

attractive all-year-round backdrop for other plants. Roses, on the whole, can look after themselves and just need fastening here and there against the wall. Climbing roses make a marvellous show, but should be sited with care in a very small space, as their prickles may become a nuisance. They grow best of all on open trellis or laths slightly away from a brick wall, because they need plenty of air around them to discourage the scourge of mildew. For a small wall the 'Lemon Pillar' rose (which is in fact white) or 'Crimson Coral Satin' is a good choice. If you prefer pink, 'Conrad F. Meyer', a rugosa rose, is a pretty one to choose. Ramblers on the other hand do just that – ramble all over the place and are not so suitable for a small area, though *Rosa filipes* 'Kiftsgate', properly trained, makes good cover.

Clematis and other 'softer' climbers, such as winter jasmine (*Jasminum nudiflorum*) and honeysuckle (*Lonicera*) will need plenty of wire, netting or trellis to cling to and climb over and to protect them from strong winds. But they do tend to make fast growth and flower quickly and they do not need tying in. They can also be grown easily in pots, as can the passion flower (*Passiflora caerulea*), which actually performs better in terms of blossoming if it has some root restriction. Try mixing roses with clematis which will scramble over the thorny branches; they go so well together.

If you are planning on climbers for pergolas and posts around a terrace, a vine, traditionally, makes an attractive network of leaves under which to dine out or sit. The most vigorous variety to choose is *Vitis vinifera* 'Brandt', which has foliage that colours in the autumn and tempting looking dark red grapes that can be used for desserts or for making wine.

North walls can be a problem, but fortunately there are a number of attractive climbers that will cope with them, notably *Hydrangea petiolaris*, which bears little or no resemblance to the ordinary hydrangea, having delicate lace-like white flowers and dark, glossy green leaves. Wisteria will also take to a north wall happily, so will the honeysuckle *Lonicera japonica*, which will give you perfume as well.

Do not be tempted to choose the tallest plant in the garden centre, take a good hard look at it first for it may be drawn out and straggly. A climber that is shorter with several stems may be a better bet and will soon catch up in height when it is in the ground. If it is container grown, make sure that it is not pot bound. Two or three roots sticking out of the bottom are probably to be expected, but you do not want a plant whose

Left A formal setpiece in a small area. The plaster plaque on the wall sets off perfectly the formal chimney-like containers and goes well with the equally formal ivy.

Pages 34 and 35 Two very different ways of dressing a wall: on the left an attractive, vigorous climber has been allowed to all but cover the brick wall of neighbouring cottages; on the right the owner of this mews cottage has settled for a variety of containers to give a patterned-wallpaper effect.

The GARDENERS PRAYER
Great God of little things
Look upon our Labours
"ke our little Gardens
A little better than our Neighbours

growth is stunted by having been too long in a pot. If you are buying plants wrapped in polythene packs, then look at them very carefully to see that they are in good condition – yellowed leaves are an indication that the plant has been sitting around on the shelf too long. Do not disturb the roots of a climber too much when you plant it; leave them in the root-ball in which they come. If the climber has come from a pack and there is no soil attached to the roots, then spread them out gently as you lower the plant into the hole you have made for it. Then firm the ground in well around it. It is a good idea to put a slug pellet or two around the base of the plant, as snails and slugs love the fresh green shoots of young climbers. Remember too that your plants will need plenty of water too.

Container-grown climbers can be put into the ground at any time of the year. Otherwise, evergreens should generally go into the ground in spring (late March or early April), while deciduous plants should be put in during their dormant winter period (between October and March).

If you are putting in a climber like wisteria around a terrace or patio or against a garden wall, it will be there to stay for a long time. Planted in a tub it will need all the help it can get. Either way a good soil with plenty of humus in it is vital. The easiest way to achieve this is to add a generous dose of peat and a little bone meal to the basic soil or compost. If you are planting against a wall you should dig out 600 mm (2 ft) square of soil about 500 mm (20 in) deep. If the soil is sticky clay, put a few stones in the bottom to help drainage and add a little lime. Never plant your climbers right up against the wall, their roots should be at least 150 mm (6 in) away, so that they have plenty of space to develop properly and get all the moisture they can. To encourage plenty of growth, you should dose your climbers with some nitrogen in late spring when they get under way and again at the end of the summer.

There are several ways of supporting climbers that need help. The quickest and easiest way is to fix plastic netting against the wall and let them scramble over that. In the case of a brick wall, you can nail in vine-eyes at intervals in the mortar between the bricks and stretch parallel wires across to take the plants. Either way, any fastenings you use must be loose enough for the plant stems to thicken up without fear of strangulation. In the case of a south-facing 'hot' wall that gets a lot of sun, the support should be fixed so that it keeps the plant away from direct contact with the wall or delicate leaves and stems may become

scorched. Plants in tubs or boxes should have a small trellis or frame of laths fixed either into the tub or onto the wall against which they stand.

If you are growing anything vigorous against the side of a building, make sure that it does not entangle itself in gutters and block them. The Russian Vine can be a culprit in this way.

Hanging gardens

Hanging gardens are a very attractive way to achieve greenery at ceiling level on a patio, a balcony or in any small back garden. It is a good idea to plant up some attractive hanging baskets and suspend them from the horizontal beams of a pergola, for instance, while the climbers that will eventually cover it are still in their infancy. Trailing ivies in attractive variegated colours or lacey leaf shapes look very good hung overhead in this way. A hanging basket needs to be really well planted, even slightly crowded with plants, if it is to have the effect you want. However, hanging baskets are inclined to be more trouble than any other container, because they usually have to be lowered to the ground for watering. So make sure all this effort is worthwhile.

Hanging baskets can also be suspended on decorative iron brackets fixed to the wall on a balcony, to make a delightful way of adding colour at a mid-height level. The easiest hanging baskets to use are those that are made like a cup and saucer: green plastic bowl with a drip-tray attached. The disadvantage of these is that you cannot poke plants in at intervals underneath, as you can with the traditional wire variety. But they do not dry out nearly as quickly, and the choice of one or two good trailing plants will soon give you colour over the side.

The traditional wire basket used in the past to be lined with sphagnum moss. But this is quite difficult to find in the shops and must be kept moist all the time or it will quickly dry off and take on an unattractive brown colour. Many people now line their baskets with black or green polythene instead, poking holes in them where needed to put in trailing plants between the wires. This works well once the plants have grown.

The average basket will take three plants from 125 mm (5 in) pots and several trailing plants. First stand the basket on a large flower pot or a bucket, so that it is held steady. Then line the basket with either a layer of sphagnum moss to a thickness of about 12 mm ($\frac{1}{2}$ in), ordinary sacking (but this will rot in time), or polythene – the dark

An informal curtain of ivy breaks the stark lines of a modern garage entrance below a period house. It parts like a bead curtain when the car is driven out.

colours look best. There is no need to put drainage material in a hanging basket. Start to fill it with John Innes Potting compost No. 3, poking any plants you want to grow out from the sides in place as you go (if you are using polythene, make slits and put the plants in place). When the basket is partly filled, set your upright plants in position. Finally, add more compost and firm it down, leaving a shallow saucer-like dip in the centre. This will collect rainwater and keep the basket from drying out too fast.

Alternatively if the basket is going to hang overhead and the top will not be seen, you can simply plant round the edges only. To help keep the moisture in you can cover the centre with a plastic saucer or a piece of polythene held down with a few pebbles.

Half baskets are filled in the same way. Half baskets placed in a regular pattern on a wall can look very attractive. Remember that hanging and wall baskets must not be put out into a garden or onto the balcony until all threat of frost is past. However, you can always get them going indoors beforehand to cheat the seasons.

Avoid hanging your baskets in places that are very exposed or in full sun or you will have to water them two or three times a day in a hot spell. Do not forget to 'dead head' them – take off dying blooms – as this will keep up the flower supply. Encourage them with an occasional liquid plant feed.

The best way to water a hanging basket is to stand it in or on a bucket and give it a good soaking. If you are planning to have really large baskets on a grand scale, it is worthwhile buying a block and tackle set from a yacht chandler's so that you can lower them to the ground when they need attention. Experiment with other hanging gardens – you could saw a large plastic bottle in half, for instance, (a freezer knife will do the trick). This can be planted up with, say, parsley and suspended with string. In a similar way very large plastic cartons can be cut in two lengthwise to make half baskets to hang on the wall by wires. You can also use a whole plastic bottle, filling it with dry soil through the top. Cut holes in it at intervals and stick small plants in, taking it down and filling it with water from time to time. A black polythene 'sausage' tube, or even a decorative plastic bag, can be filled with soil, have holes poked into it and hung up – it is fun to experiment. Even discarded wicker shopping baskets can be filled with soil, planted with flowers, and strung overhead.

There are many other ways to make walls attractive. There is no reason why you should not have shelving out of doors. Shelves make a wall into a garden instantly if you cover them with flowering plants in pots or small growing bags. This is a good way to deal with trailing plants like cucumbers and melons. For the best effect graduate the shelves so that the deepest are at the bottom and the shallowest are at the top. You must use rustproof fastenings and brackets, of course, and the wood should be painted or treated in some way to lengthen its life.

You can also buy some intriguing plant containers which interlock into each other to make a wall of their own. Such 'walls' can be placed back to back to form a free standing plant screen. Look out in your local garden centre for other imaginative ideas like this.

Opposite page A spectacular way of planting a niche. Ivy-leaved geraniums (*Pelargonium*) cascade down the wall and look particularly attractive against the rough stonework.

Left A new slant on the traditional hanging basket: a hanging trough planted with a chic one-colour theme.

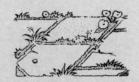

GROUND COVER

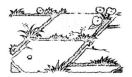

This is the age of the instant lawn. If you want one and you have a reasonably level plot, you can now buy grass by the metre, grown on a fine mesh backing. You simply unroll it, firm it into place, water it well and leave it to go on growing. It can even be put down over existing weeds provided they are not really pernicious ones like ground elder. It is not cheap, of course, but it is a worthwhile investment for a small area since it can be used immediately. Instant grass of this kind is better if you can roll it once or twice after it has been laid, but the roller on a cylinder lawnmower will do the trick over a small area. Be warned, though, that every dent and bump shows up when you lay grass like this, so try to get the area absolutely level and smooth beforehand.

Alternatively, if you are prepared to wait a little longer for the results, you can buy rolls of thin plastic foam with grass seed

Right Chamomile makes a perfect small-space alternative to a grass lawn, and emits its perfume as you tread on it. Here it has been edged with box to give a two-tone green effect.

embedded into it which you lay down, weight down, and leave to grow. The plastic foam gradually disintegrates as the young grass grows through.

For many people, however, grass is really out of the question. The space involved is too small, and in a flat or small house there is often the very practical problem of where to stow the lawnmower that is inevitably needed to go with it. This is where the grass alternatives are useful. These are plants that will give the effect of a green carpet. And once they have established themselves, a process that generally takes only a single summer, they do not need the constant attention and cutting that grass does.

Top among the grass alternatives is fragrant chamomile, much loved by the Elizabethans, which makes a splendid small

Page 40 Common thyme in bloom makes magnificent ground cover. Several different varieties can be planted together to make a multi-coloured tapestry.

lawn of deep green feathery fronds, once it has knitted together to form a carpet. It is important to get the right variety: *Anthemis nobilis* 'Treneague', which clings very closely to the ground in a dense green carpet, with unnoticeable flowers. This type never needs cutting, while traditional species of chamomile occasionally do. 'Treneague' used to be difficult to get hold of, but now, fortunately, more and more garden centres and nurserymen have it in stock. You set the plantlets 150 mm (6 in) apart and they will join together by the end of the summer to make a thick green mat.

Chamomile is more resistant to drought than grass and can be trodden on safely and it is delightfully aromatic underfoot, especially on a hot summer evening. If you do not have the space for a lawn, you might consider making a chamomile path instead. It is surprising how much punishment that these plants will take underfoot.

Raoulia tenecaulis is another good substitute for grass if you use it in a very small area. This is a plant that comes from New Zealand and it forms such a neat, flat carpet of green leaves edged with silver that it looks almost as though it has been painted on the soil beneath. You can find it at most large garden centres. Another good choice to consider is *Cotula squalida*, which has fern-like leaves rather like chamomile, but comes in a bronze-green shade.

A 'lawn' of colour

If you are dispensing with a lawn as such, then why not have a coloured carpet instead? The prostrate thymes, sub-species and varieties of the wild form *Thymus serpyllum* (which, in cultivated form, is now more correctly classified as *T. drucei*) come in all sorts of delightful colours – pinks, mauves, gold, and silver. There are around twenty different types to choose from, with different scents to match. *T. s. azoricus*, for instance, has pale mauve flowers and smells of pine. *T. s. herba-barona*, which is a little more difficult to find, has deep rose-purple flowers, tastes of caraway and was once used to flavour barons of beef, as its name implies. 'Annie Hall' has pretty very pale pink flowers. There are thymes with variegated gold and silver leaves, and some of them have quite different woolly, grey-green leaves – 'Pink Chintz', for instance. You will find a good selection of these thymes at most herb farms and also at any nursery or garden centre specializing in rock garden or alpine plants, for they make good plants for rockeries and crevices too. Thymes like plenty of sun, so do not plant

Left Pinks and other 'pin-cushion' plants look splendid if planted between paving stones, adding colour here and there all summer through.

43

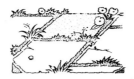

them in a shady area, and they must have a basically well-drained soil. If you have a shade to cope with, then plant wild white clover (*Trifolium repens*), which seems to thrive in dark situations – you can even put it under trees where virtually nothing else will grow. White clover has an ornamental variety, 'Purpurascens Quadriphyllum', which has an attractive purplish foliage. However, its colour will be barely distinguishable from the parent species if it is planted in deep shade.

Ground cover for all places

What makes a good ground cover plant? It needs to be relatively strong to overcome weeds and it needs to be sturdy enough to form a carpet fairly quickly, when it will do a useful job of keeping moisture in the ground. Ideally it should be an evergreen plant, but failing that it should have something of interest to offer at some time of the year – not necessarily attractive flowers but perhaps variegated or brightly coloured foliage or fruit. It should also be something that needs little or no maintenance apart from a trim. Having said that, it should be emphasised that there are

several kinds of ground-covering plants which do need time and trouble taken over them. But such plants bring their rewards. For example, a clematis planted as a ground cover will eventually produce an area of attractive flowers.

Some of these plants make a carpet by rooting themselves in the ground as they grow – chamomile is one of these. Others tend to form hummocks and are better used between stones and in crevices. Lady's mantle (*Alchemilla mollis*) is one of these with its pretty sprays of greeny-yellow flowers. Then there are spreaders like the wild snow-in-summer, or dusty miller (*Cerastium tomentosum*), which grows rapidly to form a silvery mat; and creepers and twiners which will, in time, make a mass of tangled cover over a flower bed. Finally, there are trailing lobelias, notably the trailing or Pendula varieties of *Lobelia erinus*, which are useful as ground cover in pots, tubs, and window-boxes and which trail decoratively over the edges of these and other containers.

Sedums have fleshy leaves and go well in rather stark surroundings, the flowers are rosette-like and come in many colours. If you want a really fast grower, then look for

Opposite page Instant ground cover: this paved area has been decorated by plants in pots that can be switched around at will. The hostas and hydrangeas here add extra interest with their foliage.

Below *Lobelia* 'String of Pearls' provides colourful, attractive ground cover during the summer months, making a perfect foil for some of the larger shrubs.

Sedum spurium 'Ruby Mantle' which has deep red-purple foliage and rosy pink flowers. Houseleeks (*Sempervivum*) are hardy succulents that make good ground cover in stone troughs or sinks. Some of them throw up flowers on columns of leaves, and like most succulents they prefer a dry, sunny position. Another good choice to plant between paving stones is thrift (*Armeria*), which makes pincushion-like hummocks.

Many of the plants listed as alpines make good carpeting plants, not only as lawn substitutes but also for filling cracks and crevices between paving. Dull concrete slabs, for instance, can be livened up if you plant alpines such as *Acaena buchananii*, which makes a silvery grey mat, or some of the sedums such as *Sedum album* 'Coral Carpet' which, as its name suggests, has reddish foliage and pink flowers, too. Sedums, also known as stonecrops, are like thyme – they prefer well-drained soil and plenty of sun, and their flowers are particularly attractive to butterflies. If you select carefully you can find sedum varieties that bloom all summer and into the autumn. Plant *S. spectabile* 'Autumn Joy' for blue-green leaves with pink flowers which appear about September and gradually darken to brown. If you want a carpeter, choose *S. spurium* 'Green Mantle' which is evergreen that bears no flowers and spreads rapidly.

Aubrieta (*Aubrieta deltoidea*) makes a cheap and cheerful choice of plant to be grown over the edge of a low wall or between paving. It is very easy to grow from seed, and cultivars vary in colour from 'Triumphant', which is a true blue, to 'Bob Saunders', which is a lesser-known variety with large double reddish-purple flowers, and the very popular 'Dr Mules', which has flowers of deep violet. Aubrietas need to be cut right back at the end of the season or they will produce patches of unattractive dark brown matting.

Alyssum can be grown easily from seed too, but avoid, if you can, the ordinary white or purple *Alyssum maritimum* and look for its cultivar 'Wonderland', which has deep red flowers, or for gold dust (*A. saxatile*), of which 'Citrinum', which has bright yellow flowers and the low-growing, golden yellow 'Compactum' are among the best. They are more difficult to track down, but are well worth the effort.

Think, too, in terms of edible ground cover, especially in large tubs. Alpine strawberries varieties of *Fragaria vesca* grow very rapidly and give you a double bonus in terms of fruit as well as coverage.

'Baron Solemacher' is one of the best known varieties. It is a very strong grower and gives heavy crops of bright red sweet fruit from May to September.

Chives (*Allium schoenoprasum*) can be used as a grass substitute in a tub or a sink. Keep it well snipped to encourage it to spread, and do not let the plants form flower-heads or the leaves will lose their pungency. Marjoram, too, will cover an area in a surprisingly short time. Choose French golden marjoram for the prettiest effect. It has gold-green leaves and pink flowers. If you are using marjoram as a carpeter, then try mixing three types – common marjoram (*Origanum vulgare*) which has pink flowers, French golden, and sweet or knotted marjoram (*O. marjorana*), otherwise known as oregano, which has grey-green leaves and white flowers.

If you are starting from scratch and are planning to put down some sort of firm base, such as paving, in a small back yard, consider making a 'chequerboard' of alternate squares of paving stones and soil. The squares between the paving can be planted with multicoloured alpines. Apart from the kinds already mentioned, consider some of the pretty Alpine phloxes, such as *Phlox subulata* 'Benita', which has lavender-mauve flowers, or *P. douglasii* 'May Snow', which gives you a carpet of white. Everlasting flower (*Helichrysum*), comes in an alpine version too – *H. bellidioides*. Tiny alpines like this look particularly attractive if you scatter the surface of the soil between them with tiny pebbles or gravel.

In a patio garden or a back yard, ground cover can be used very effectively to underplant small flowerbeds and give you double value out of the space. The fact that you are using ground cover here mainly to smother weeds does not mean that it need be dull. All the climbers and trailers from clematis and passion flower (*Passiflora caerulea*) to annuals such as morning glory (*Ipomoea*) can be used as ground cover with great success, together with closer-covering plants like the greater periwinkle (*Vinca major*). However, remember to put down slug and snail pellets when planting them this way.

Two of the evergreen clematis make excellent ground cover: *Clematis armandii*, with shiny dark-green leaves and tiny white flowers in spring; and *C. balearicci*, which has ferny foliage that turns a bronze shade in winter and bears pale yellow flowers in early spring. They are not as closely knit as some of the more traditional ground cover plants, but they look very attractive and can be combined with a more sober cover, such

Edible ground cover at its best: the popular Alpine strawberry variety 'Baron Solemacher' will grow happily in the shade of evergreens and will fruit throughout the summer.

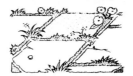

as a green-leaved ivy. Variegated ivies can also be used, of course. *Hedera canariensis* 'Variegata', for instance, has silver-edged leaves. If you feel confident that you can keep it in check, the Russian vine (*Polygonum baldschuanicum*) will smother anything in a short space of time.

Herbs also make good ground cover. Mint, for instance, provided that it is mixed with shrubs rather than with herbaceous plants, grows very rapidly indeed and if you choose a version like white variegated or ginger mint (*Mentha × gentilis*), which has bright yellow stripes, it can look very attractive. Keep cutting mints back so that they will spread quickly. There are dozens of varieties to choose from – eau-de-cologne and orange mints, for instance, or water mint (*Mentha aquatica*) for damp places. Mints prefer a sunny site, and be careful not to allow the soil to dry out in summer.

Other good ground-covering plants include the lavenders. Dutch lavender (*Lavandula vera*) and its cultivar 'Nana Alba', which has white flowers, are both good choices. Do not despise honeysuckle in its bushy form: *Lonicera pileata* has attractive purple fruits in autumn and makes a good ground cover in the larger garden.

A semi-evergreen, it will grow happily in deep shade under trees.

In a simple modern backyard, an unusual form of ground cover in a permanent planting could be one of the prostrate conifers, such as *Juniperus procumbens* and its variety 'Nana', which look good as an underplanting among large bushes or trees.

Raised beds, tubs, and window-boxes

Raised beds can have their ground cover too, and this is a good opportunity to use plants with small flowers so that you can see them. Snow-in-summer (*Cerastium tomentosum* or *C. biebersteinii*) forms dense mats of silver leaves very quickly and looks good when used for ground cover in this way; but it needs keeping in check or it will get out of hand. Dwarf lavenders are also useful. In summer scented-leaved geraniums (*Pelargonium*) used as bedding plants spread quickly, but they need to be brought in before the first frosts arrive. On the other hand, they will provide scent indoors in winter.

Ground cover for tubs and window-boxes plays a double role, it adds to the

Alpines provide permanent ground cover for a no-fuss garden. Here the prostrate juniper, *Juniperus procumbens*, gives dense coverage.

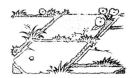

colour and it helps to keep moisture in. It can be more showy than that used for beds. Trailing blue lobelias (*Lobelia erinus* varieties) are old favourites that are easy to obtain. 'Pendula Blue Cascade' has the deepest blue flowers, while 'Pendula Sapphire' has blue flowers with white eyes in them. Look out, too, for the red cultivars of *L. fulgens* from America; 'Red Cascade' has crimson flowers with white centres. You can raise them from seed and with luck they will give you flowers all summer until the first frosts. For a change, try *L. erinus* 'Crystal Palace', which has bronze foliage rather than the usual green, and is a good choice if you are planting in the shade.

Do not forget the very useful nasturtiums (*Tropaeolum*), which are so easy to grow and do not need raising in a seed tray – just sow some seeds in tubs and leave them to it. Their trumpet flowers are usually in orange-yellow shades, but look out for some of the newer hybrids which produce colours ranging from salmon pink to crimson; you can have them in creamy white, too. If you want to avoid too much sprawl, go for the dwarf varieties.

Some of the traditional cottage-garden flowers make good underplanting in large tubs. Forget-me-not (*Myosotis*), for instance, is a biennial and needs raising from seed sown the previous summer (or you can buy it as a bedding-out plant). Baby-blue-eyes (*Nemophila menziesii*) is an easily grown annual that has buttercup-shaped blue flowers with white centres. Wallflowers (*Cheiranthus*) are inclined to be straggly, but look pretty when planted with forget-me-nots; while candytuft (*Iberis*) and creeping jenny (*Lysimachia nummularia*) have white and yellow flowers respectively. Starry white baby's breath (*Gypsophila*) comes in a prostrate form – *G. repens* – and looks pretty as an underplanting for more colourful flowers.

Even the smallest pot can have its own ground cover. A plant such as mind-your-own-business or baby's tears (*Helxine soleirolii*), which comes from Corsica, makes a tiny carpet in either pale green or even paler green-yellow. It has strange flowers like tiny coral beads. It is not totally hardy and should be planted permanently only in very sheltered spots or in pots that will be taken indoors in the winter. Another unusual ground cover plant is Corsican mint (*Mentha requenii*), which has tiny, darkish green leaves. It loathes dry conditions,

Instant, uncomplicated ground cover from June to September is provided by the cheap and cheerful nasturtium. Dwarf forms are available if you need low-growing plants.

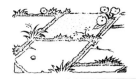

however, and must be kept well watered, especially during the summer, if it is to survive. If you want something slightly larger and hardier, choose the pungent 'pennyroyal' (*M. pulegium*) instead.

Looking after ground cover

However fast they grow, all plants used as ground cover need help during the first few months. It is important to remove weeds, however tiny, that may spring up between young plants that have not yet developed into a mat. The easiest way to do this is by hand or with a kitchen fork, but try not to disturb the ground-cover plant in any way. If you are planting really tiny, delicate plants, such as mind-your-own-business or Corsican mint, it is a good idea to put a sheet of black polythene down, cutting holes to let the plants poke through until they have spread to form larger clumps. This has the double advantage of keeping in moisture and smothering any weeds.

Well-established ground cover plants will hardly ever need watering. Be sure, however, to shade the roots of clematis from strong sun; pieces of tile around the base of the stem will suffice. To encourage climbers of this kind to act instead as ground cover, peg the shoots down at intervals with large hairpins. Carpeting plants that get out of hand can be cut back and thinned; the rooted pieces you remove can be used to start colonies elsewhere.

Small areas

Faced with a roof garden, patio, or balcony which is not suitable for growing grass or one of the substitutes, what can be done to make it look more attractive? On a concreted patio a fake 'carpet' of ceramic tiles looks attractive; you could consider tiling only part of the area. A balcony or a roof garden that is covered in bituminous material may become unpleasantly tacky in high summer. You can tile such an area as long as you are sure that it can stand the extra weight. But the best way to cover the sticky surface is to buy some lightweight wooden duckboarding of the kind that is used on yachts. This enables you to walk about without getting tar on your shoes. Duckboarding is relatively easy to make up from wooden laths and runners. Also available is duckboarding with a plastic surface, which can be wiped clean.

Alternatively, you can have fun with fake grass, which you lay just like carpet. It can be used outdoors or in and looks particularly good when you put it either side

of a set of French doors, so bringing the balcony or garden into the room. There are several kinds to choose from, giving different thicknesses of pile and several shades of green. Fake grass is guaranteed against fading in sunlight, although a carelessly dropped lighted cigarette will burn a hole in it. Fake grass is basically waterproof and little or no water should drain through it. It can be cleaned with a vacuum cleaner or hosed and cleaned with detergent – it dries quickly. It can be left permanently in situ, or it may be rolled up and brought indoors when not in use.

Another cheap idea is rush matting or split-cane matting, both of which look good on a balcony or a roof garden and lend it a Mediterranean air. Split-cane matting rolls up easily and stows away in a corner of a cupboard. Both these types of ground covering look good with deckchairs or cane chairs and a surrounding of brilliantly coloured flowers such as petunias.

Opposite page This somewhat sparsely planted centre bed in a small garden is filled out and given extra height and greater variety by the addition of pots of herbs.

Below Not all lawns need to be cut. In this small roof garden, fake grass in the form of plastic turfing provides a touch of green under foot.

BASIC CONTAINERS

The most instant garden of all is the one you plant in containers. Buy a window-box (or build your own) or get a tub from your local garden centre or shop, add a bag of compost and a tray of bedding plants in flower and in a very short time you have colour right on your window-sill.

There is a lot to be said for container gardening. There is no heavy digging to do; you do not even have to bend down if your container is sited high enough; there is little or no weeding to worry about; and you are less troubled by weather conditions than in a conventional plot.

You can suit yourself as far as soil is concerned, filling some pots with the acid kind for lime-hating plants such as rhododendrons and azaleas and others with chalky soil, which clematis and fuchsias love. In short, you have the best of all gardening worlds.

You can also shift your garden around in any way you want, provided that you have made sure that your containers are movable. You can give them each a turn to have their fair share of the sun. You can tuck ones that have finished flowering behind the others, or use planted containers to hide an unattractive feature.

The range of containers that can be used is enormous. Anything from a cocoa tin to a giant tub can be used to hold plants. Surprisingly large trees can be container-grown too – some are planted in city streets in this way – and you can even have a mini-orchard of fruit trees and vines in large containers on a permanent basis, provided you feed them well.

Generally, it is more labour-saving to put several plants into one large container rather than have them arranged singly in an array of pots. They grow better together, they need watering less frequently, and they make a greater visual impact: one large tub looks much more impressive and takes up less space than half a dozen flower pots huddled together.

Choosing containers

Containers are made in several different kinds of material and it is important to choose the material that suits both you and your garden. Plastic saves the most labour and it is usually cheapest, too. It is lightweight, colour-fast, and, unless it gets cracked or torn, will last for a long time, although it tends to get brittle after several years in the sunlight.

Since particles of earth and dust are less likely to cling to their smooth sides, plastic containers are easily wiped clean. They are

also water-tight, so plants in such containers need watering less often than those in conventional clay pots. You can easily pierce as many drainage holes as you need into the base; most plastic pots and boxes now come with punch-out drainage holes already positioned in them, making the work easier still – a light tap with a hammer on the top of a screwdriver or small chisel will usually do the trick.

Plastic containers are now being made in some attractive classic shapes, ranging in appearance from imitation wood to plain white and in some good colours, too. If you

do not like the shades, it is easy to change the colour and repaint the pot available at your local garden centre or flower shop, yourself, using an acrylic-based paint for the job.

Large-size plastic buckets also make good small tubs (it is easy to take off their handles). Alternatively, they can be put inside larger, more decorative containers and used as tub liners, which is a useful trick if you are planning to switch your plants around, and also allows you to use attractive but non-water-tight containers.

Glass fibre is similar to plastic, but there are important differences. It is more brittle

than most plastics and should be handled with a certain amount of care; it can in some circumstances chip or split. It is also very expensive, but should, if handled properly, last for a life-time. If you want a 'period' look for your pots, this is your best choice, as glass-fibre can be used to simulate any container material from wood to lead.

Stone, artificial stone, and concrete containers look very attractive, but they are very heavy, so you should be sure where you want to site them before you plant them up. They are expensive, too, and tend to be fragile: they may crack in a heavy frost or crumble with age, so they should never be moved unless it is absolutely necessary. Among the newest designs is an interlocking series of plant pots, constructed of glass-reinforced cement, which make a low, free-standing wall. You can make concrete containers of a variety of shapes and sizes by using timber formwork 'moulds'.

Terracotta pots, including the traditional flower pot, look and feel good, but they tend to break easily and need watering frequently, since moisture evaporates through them. Plants grown in such containers are also more likely to have their roots affected by frost, so they need more attention, and it is a good idea to protect them in really cold weather. With all these drawbacks, however, terracotta pots do look somehow sympathetic with plants.

Wooden containers have the disadvantage that they tend to deteriorate over a period of time, however thoroughly you paint them or treat them with preservative. However, wood is invaluable for purpose-built containers – a special size of box to fit a difficult window-sill for instance, or a wooden tub to fit in an awkward corner. Wooden tubs or half-barrels are fairly heavy; they also lose water easily – in summer a tub on a hot patio may need watering as often as two or three times a day.

You may be lucky enough to lay your hands on a cheap large tub or a half-barrel that has been used for some other purpose. It is essential to make sure that the tub is thoroughly cleaned before you use it. Soak it first with plain water, allowing the wood to take up moisture, then scrub the inside with a strong solution of permanganate of potash; put the tub on plastic sheeting first as the permanganate will leave a mauve stain that is difficult to eradicate. Then treat the outside of the tub with a preservative to prevent rot.

Look for unusual items for containers. An old wooden wheelbarrow piled with

Even a small and dark basement area responds to a spot of white paint, which not only brightens it up but helps to reflect more light on those plants out of direct sunlight. Here containers ranging from teapots to paint cans are pressed into service to house flowering plants.

pots of geraniums adds a new dimension to a small backyard or patio. Old kitchen coppers can be planted very attractively, as can really large, canteen-sized kettles. Precious pots need not have drainage holes punched in them: you simply sit each plant in a plastic flower pot inside. Old kitchen sinks make good troughs for small plants such as alpines. Stone sinks can be left as they are, but china clay ones look better if you give them a rough-cast treatment. Spread them first with impact-bonding PVA glue (you will need rubber gloves for this job), then pat on a mixture of Portland cement, sand, and peat in proportions of

need a minimum distance of 150 mm (6 in) between the surface of the soil and the drainage layer.

Small-sized and odd-shaped containers will often go in unexpected places. You can position them down the side of outside steps or a fire escape, for instance, and plant them with scented-leaved geraniums (*Pelargonium*) that perfume the air as you brush past them. Miniature roses look very attractive if planted in small containers on a window-sill, where they can be better appreciated than if they are in the ground.

A temporary container for growing, say, tomato plants, is a plastic growing-bag,

Large, unorthodox containers need to be carefully sited. This one, by a front door in a regency terrace, complements the formal lines of the architecture.

$1:2\frac{1}{2}:1\frac{1}{2}$ over the sides and leave it to dry. Do not try to put on too much rough cast at a time. The best way is to build up the thickness of the coating by making several applications, allowing the rough cast to dry between each application.

Right at the other end of the scale, if cash is limited, you can save your money for plants by copying the Mediterranean French and Italians. Collect together the largest-sized cans you can find and plant those (do not forget the drainage holes in the bottom). You can spray or paint them all the same colour with a lacquer. Remember that for proper root growth almost all plants will

which comes ready-filled with compost. It is commonly of a rather garish colour, but if it is placed on the ground, you can disguise its side edges with a frame of floor boards nailed together, or two or three rows of dry-laid bricks.

All containers, whatever their material or shape, should be kept just off the ground they are standing on. This will discourage the roots of the plants from poking through in search of more moisture or nourishment, and it will also help to keep out unwelcome pests like earwigs, slugs, and snails from making their homes underneath. Raised containers, in any case, are often much more

attractive, since the plants can be seen more easily. Small containers can be put on pieces of broken tile or flower pot; larger containers can perch on bricks or, better still, have castors fitted to them so they can be moved around.

Really large containers should be moved as little as possible, of course, for it can take the united efforts of three or four people to shift them and the plants inside may be damaged. If you do have to move your container, the easiest make-shift way is to tip the container up onto one of its bottom edges and slip a strong sack or stout piece of material under it. Then you can drag the

An attractive country planting: ferns and begonias have been allowed to rampage unchecked over an old stone sink.

sack, with the container sitting on it, to the new position.

The best time to move large containers is at the time of year when you are replacing at least part of the soil. Alternatively, if you have a porter's trolley, you can slide the container onto that, making sure it is seated snugly against the frame at the back before you tilt the trolley back and wheel it away. In a garden that has a number of large containers it is well worth while making a 'dolly', a low, flat platform fitted with castors. The plants must be jolted as little as possible when they are being moved.

Window-boxes

Some very attractive window-boxes are now available in plastic and glass-fibre but, being mass-produced, they come in standard sizes – usually between 600 and 750 mm (2 and 3 ft) long and 225 mm (9 in) wide. Before investing in one check that your window-sill is not only long enough for it but also wide enough. Check also that the windows will not knock the plants when they are opened. Casement windows do not rule out window-boxes altogether, but the latter will almost certainly have to be fixed on

stout brackets below sill level. Do not place a window-box on too narrow a sill; and make sure that it is in a sheltered position. For safety you should screw the box onto the window frame or put a permanent guard rail in front. Remember that a window cleaner, for instance, might well grab hold of the box to steady himself, and that strong winds can move quite heavy things. You need to think carefully, too, before positioning a box over a doorway without a porch: it may drip onto callers awaiting entry.

Attractive wooden window-boxes do not have to be bought; they are quite easy to make. Old floor boards can sometimes be found for the job, but any hardwood that is at least 25 mm (1 in) thick can be used. Excellent window-boxes can be made from furniture such as old tables, wardrobes, or drawers. Softwood *can* be used, but it will not last for more than three or four years, even with great care. Never make a window-box without treating the timber well in advance against woodworm, and dosing it with a preservative. Creosote should never be used, as it is poisonous and may damage the plants. A proprietary version of copper naphthenate solution is the best choice; you can get it from garden centres.

Young bamboo plants, given a temporary home in this window-box, provide a fern-like display of greenery.

Your window-box should have sufficient depth to plant a reasonable variety of plants and, perhaps, some all-year-round dwarf shrubs, too. It should be at least 175 mm (7 in) deep inside when finished – 300 mm (12 in) is even better and gives you more scope – and it should be 225 mm (9 in) wide. Use zinc-plated or brass screws to fix the pieces together to prevent rust, and make sure that the short side pieces fit inside the longer front and back planks so that no rough edges show.

The box should have hooks or brackets screwed to it so that it can be anchored to the window-sill, and it will almost certainly need front legs longer than the back ones to level it up, as most window-sills slope. Cotton reels are quite good for this purpose. Drainage holes should be about 12.5 mm ($\frac{1}{2}$ in) in diameter in the average-sized box and be arranged about 150 mm (6 in) apart in a zigzag pattern. And, if moisture in the box is at all likely to drip on people below, stand it on a shallow tray.

Plants for containers

Putting in tubs and troughs increases the scope and flexibility of your garden

scheme. You can, for instance, plant any number of trees and some of the more vigorous climbers, such as wisteria, in containers. Clematis can also be planted in a tub, but it may need its own climbing frame, and the tub should be well shaded so that the roots do not get too hot.

Tubs and troughs are in many ways more on display than window-boxes, which are more likely to form part of a general scheme. So they need to fit in with the mood of their surroundings. Fortunately, there is such a wide choice available that this is no problem. A container does need, however, to be light in weight and easily portable if you intend to move it around. At the same time it needs to be fairly rigid or the roots of the plant growing inside may be disturbed when the container is moved. Be sure that each container suits the proportions of the plant it is designed to go with. A huge tub with one small plant cowering in the middle is a waste of space. It is better to wait until the shrub has grown up a little before investing in a large container. Avoid planting tall, floppy herbaceous plants that need staking; it is much better to choose dwarf versions of flowers such as Michaelmas daisies (*Aster*).

Even small areas such as window-boxes can feature a mixture of permanent and short-term plantings. Here miniature conifers, standing sentinel all year round, make a perfect back-drop for colourful busy lizzie in the summer.

Specimen container-grown plants have a luxury life compared with those in a garden bed, for they are bound to get special treatment. They are not competing for space and they are usually under constant scrutiny and are therefore less likely to be seriously damaged by pests or diseases before their plight is spotted. But containers are expensive to buy in the first place, so it is important that you get the best value from them. In particular, you should plan to plant them up in such a way as to provide something interesting and colourful to look at all year round.

Evergreen trees are best on patios and balconies: the naked branches of most deciduous trees look unattractive in winter. One tub, for instance, could have a dwarf cypress surrounded in spring by daffodils and crocuses, and in summer by bedding plants like geraniums, which will last until the first frosts. It could also include an underplanting of trailing lobelia. Another good permanent subject for a tub or trough is an azalea (make sure you have the right acid soil mix). If you want to do something a little different, think in terms of using tubs in unconventional ways; make the most of money spent on special plants, for instance, by grouping them closely together. Lilies look majestic in a tub, as do tulips and tiger flowers (*Tigridia*).

Growing mediums

Soil used in window-boxes and tubs is going to be worked far harder than normal garden soil, so never skimp. The best soil for containers and window-boxes is a purpose-mixed one, such as John Innes No 3 compost. If you have garden soil to hand and have a large container to fill, then put soil in first and fill up with the compost. The nutrients in the compost will gradually soak down as the plant is watered. If weight is a problem – and it may well be in the case of a balcony or roof garden – consider using vermiculite (which consists of feather-light grains of silica) instead of soil, or choose one of the peat-based composts which are very light in weight.

A point to bear in mind when going out to buy compost is to check whether or not it contains added fertilizer; if it does, you could over-feed your plants by adding more. One snag about using a peat compost is that it is surprisingly difficult to get it thoroughly wet – a necessary thing to do when you are planting. Water hosed over peat will just run through it; so instead, use a fine spray, watering it slowly until the top is soaked. For the same reason, never allow

If a window sill is too shallow to accommodate a window-box, a shelf of identical containers painted the same colour creates a sophisticated effect in a town setting.

The Versailles tub, which was once used to house orange trees, makes an excellent container for small formal trees and shrubs or for climbers trained up a cane.

If carefully selected for colour and form, widely different plants can benefit from being grouped together in one container instead of in several small ones. Here a large decorative tub makes a home for an attractive mix of plants.

peat-based compost to dry out completely.

Peat is usually very dark in colour and this can delude you into thinking it is damp when it is in fact dry. So test the surface frequently by touch, rather than go by appearances. If you are using peat or any other lightweight, non-soil compost you will not need drainage crocks in the bottom of the container; but you must remember that this kind of growing medium tends to pack down in time and will need topping up with fresh compost.

The advantage of using special compost or peat is that it is sterile: it should be completely free of the weed seeds that are usually present in ordinary soil. Against that you have the cost involved, but if you can invest in purpose-mixed compost you know your plants will be off to a good start: all the right nutrients will be present and harmful insects, weeds, and bacteria will be absent. You can mix your own compost, of course, by buying leafmould, garden sand, and loam by the bag, but this is a messy business in a small space.

If you want to move your plants around, the most flexible way to do this is to keep them growing in fairly small pots and plunge them into larger containers filled with vermiculite or some other lightweight, soil-less compost. In this way you can keep a show of colour going all the year round, raising cheap colourful annuals in seed trays indoors, pricking them out into pots, and putting them in place just as they are about to burst into bloom.

Planting

Keeping the drainage holes free is a vital part of successful planting, because the roots of plants need air, just as the stems and leaves do, and this air is contained in tiny pockets in the soil. When you water a container or a window-box, the water soaks through the soil and some of it drains out the other end, pulling down behind it fresh supplies of air through the soil.

For good drainage, first place a layer – about 50 mm (2 in) thick in the case of a standard window-box or a tub – of broken brick, washed cinders, or broken crocks in for drainage. Broken pieces of clay flower pot are ideal for this. If you are using pieces of brick, make sure that there is no lime-based mortar clinging to them that might offend acid-loving plants. Over the crocks put a layer of damp peat, and, if the container is to be planted up permanently, include a few pieces of charcoal to keep the soil sweet (charcoal from a barbecue pack is excellent for this job). Then top up the

This basketful of vivid geraniums (*Pelargonium*) placed against an old timbered door makes a fascinating study in texture as well as colours.

container with the appropriate compost.

Some circumstances dictate variations on this basic plan. As already noted, if you are using a peat-based compost, you will not need drainage crocks because the water would drain away all too easily. However, if the compost is very small grained and the drainage holes are large, it is a wise precaution to put a piece of broken crock over each of the holes to stop the compost being washed through. You may find, incidentally, that a light-weight compost such as vermiculite has a tendency to be blown away. If that happens, sprinkle some granite chippings or gravel on top to help anchor it down.

If you are planting a container in mid-summer, it is a good idea to push corks into one or two of the drainage holes. In hot weather this will help conserve water, and the corks can be taken out later on. If it is a rainy time of year, make sure that the holes are completely clear and that they have plenty of drainage material over them. If the soil becomes compacted and waterlogged, it will be completely deprived of air; the roots can rot away without your realizing it. The first indication you have of this is that the plant suddenly keels over.

In an ideal patio garden there should be both summer and winter containers. The summer ones should have drainage holes in the sides, about 25 mm (1 in) up from the base, but none in the bottom, this will ensure that, with regular watering, there is always a reserve of water in the containers. The winter containers should have holes only in the bottom. If you are making a long-term garden, then it is worth while having different containers for each season. Or you could make two sets of holes in your containers and plug them alternately as the seasons change.

Planting a strawberry barrel

A decorative barrel planted with strawberries, herbs, or flowers is a very attractive feature. But it can be surprisingly heavy, so it is well worth going to the expense of mounting the barrel on castors before you start. Then it can be turned from time to time to make sure that each side gets its share of sunlight – important when fruit is ripening.

Strawberry barrels need a special drainage system. First, make sure there are drainage holes in the base and, if it does not already have holes in the sides, you will need to cut 50 mm (2 in) holes in a diamond pattern. When you are ready to fill the barrel, first place the usual minimum 50 mm

(2 in) layer of broken crocks in the bottom. Make sure at this stage that the barrel is standing absolutely level, otherwise you will have trouble both in filling it and in watering it. If it is leaning at an angle, some plants will never receive moisture and others will almost drown.

Now stand a piece of plastic drainpipe upright in the middle of the barrel (it pays to have someone to help you at this stage) and hold it in place while you fill the pipe with shingle or pebbles and the barrel with soil, keeping the two level as you go. Every time the soil level reaches a hole in the side of the barrel, poke a plant through the hole and firm the soil down around it. When the barrel is about half full, gradually start raising the pipe up as you continue to fill.

Opposite page
Strawberry barrels can be used with great decorative effect – and not only for strawberry plants. This painted barrel makes a focal point for a formal bed.

Below Use containers of flowers as spot colour in a garden. They can be grouped together to provide major points of interest, or they can be sited individually to brighten up drab areas.

Then it is easy to pull it out altogether once you have finished. Large strawberry or herb pots can be treated in very much the same way, using a cardboard tube and small-size shingle. The central drainage core ensures that water and fertilizer are carried down to all levels.

Maintenance

Container-grown plants need regular grooming if they are to look good. Pick off dead leaves, and snip off blossoms the moment they fade in order to encourage the development of more. Do not leave debris around the surface of the soil; it is likely to attract disease organisms. Put it on the compost heap, if you have the space for one, or put it in the dustbin. Plants with shiny, leathery leaves should be cleaned regularly if they are growing in town conditions, and especially if they are evergreens. Bay trees, in particular, respond to this treatment. The best way to treat them is to sponge them down with water to which a drop (no more) of detergent has been added, then rinse them with plain water. You could also give them a foliar feed from time to time and, as a cosmetic treatment, spray them with a leaf shine. (Some gardeners sponge them with a mixture of milk and water to make them gleam.) Do not tackle any of these jobs if the plant will be placed in strong sunlight; tiny droplets of liquid on the leaves will act like magnifying glasses and burn them.

Check your containers for rust, loose joints, or cracks, depending on the material from which they are made, and give plastic pots and troughs an occasional wipe-over to smarten them up. If your containers are well planted, there should not be any space available for weeds, but if these do appear, hook them out as soon as possible – they are stealing food from the soil and may also deny your plants light.

Feeding

Container-grown plants should be fed at flowering time, when they are being worked hard. It is particularly important to make sure they are well drained at this time or you will have an excessive build up of fertilizer in the soil.

For the first month after planting, container-grown plants can be left without feeding, provided that you have used a good compost mix. After that a fortnightly liquid feed will keep them in perfect condition. However, in the case of some quick-growing flowering plants, such as nasturtiums and marigolds, it is best to avoid

Even outward-opening casement windows can have window-boxes provided the latter are fitted below sill level. In this scheme, a colourful framing effect is achieved by the pots fixed on either side of the window.

feeding them until they start to flower or you may get a great deal of green leaf and no blooms. Make sure that the surface of the soil is damp before you apply fertilizer so that it is distributed properly.

Watering

Plants in an exposed position will need more watering than those in the shelter of a wall or in the shade, so bear this fact in mind in warm weather. Be prepared to water your plants twice a day in summer if they are in a hot position or if they are in small containers. Hanging baskets in particular dry out very quickly indeed, so it is a good idea to fix them on a pulley so they can be lowered into a bucket of water for a soak – the easiest way of watering them.

Collect rainwater if you can; your prize plants will appreciate it. Water in the early morning or at dusk, never when the sun is shining on the plants. Use a rose rather than a jet, for the latter may break tender plants, stir up the surface of the soil too vigorously, or damage delicate roots near the surface.

Over-watering is seldom a problem for plants that are growing out of doors unless drainage is bad and containers become waterlogged. If you are at all worried about this, a moisture meter is a good investment. This will keep you accurately informed about the moisture content of the soil.

If you have to go away for some time and there is no one to water your plants, then capillary matting is the best answer. You can buy this matting at any garden centre. Place the plants on a bed of this with an end or a corner dipped into a large bucket or tin bath of water. The plant pots will then soak up water as they need it through the matting. Window-boxes respond well to a trickle watering system if you are away for a very short time and have a handy tap available. Simply puncture a piece of hose pipe at regular intervals and lay the punctured length along the surface of a window-box. Attach one end of the hose to a dripping tap and stop up the other end: the water that seeps out of the holes will keep your window-box moist while you are away.

Finally, as a temporary measure, black polythene laid over the soil surface of a tub containing shrubs or trees will help keep moisture in. Be sure to anchor it with a stone or two and tuck the edges into the soil, otherwise strong winds may wrap it around the plant instead.

QUICK COLOUR

Bedding out – the putting in of half-hardy annual flowers in spring – was an occupation much loved by the Victorians, who had plenty of gardening staff to call upon. Unfortunately more and more bedding plants are now being banished from conventional gardens because of the work involved – digging and hoeing the border, putting in the rows of plants – and the relatively high cost.

In an instant garden, however, consisting of a window-box, a container, or just one narrow bed around the edge of a patio, bedding plants are invaluable for spot colour and are a method of making a few plants go a long way. Used in a small space, they give you a shower of flowers near the house for a relatively low cost. Bedding plants can be bought quite cheaply, especially if you go to the local markets for them, and they give some of the best short-term value for money you can have – less than a pound will buy you a row of lobelias, for instance, which will make a cascade down the edge of a pot all summer.

Think of your display as if you are painting a picture and arrange it accordingly. You can use the colours of flowers to create an illusion, to make a plot or a window-box look cool or warm for instance. Some people believe that natural flower colours do not clash, but this is debatable. Some of the brighter petunias, for instance, tend to 'fight' with geraniums and cause an unsettling effect. Generally, blues and mauves look best next to pale yellows and pinks, while the same yellows will give quite a different effect alongside bronze or red. Red lilacs and purples together can look rather hot – but that may be the very effect you need to achieve in a shaded corner which needs brightening up, so that the flowers look like a coal fire.

Silver-leaved plants are very useful for cooling down hot-coloured plants. White flowers look best either heightened by silver or backed by dark rather than light green leaves.

It is important to plan a succession of colour all through the summer rather than to aim for just one fortnight of splendour. You should, therefore, avoid plants that need a long lead time before they flower. Shape, too, needs thinking about. In a tub tall, spiky plants like delphiniums should be placed in the centre, with other, shorter plants around them, graduating down to trailers over the edge. In a border it is best to put the tallest plants at the back. Not only will they be protected from the wind but also they will not obscure other plants.

Remember, too, that you can plan for

The border in this tiny front garden has been crammed with carefully positioned plants and makes a striking blend of formality and colour.

Page 74 An instant summer show to brighten up a window: petunias, trailing lobelias, and pelargoniums can always be relied upon to give splashes of colour.

scent as well as colour: a scented window-box is a delight on a summer night, and you can 'bed out' your flowering houseplants in summer for extra colour. Do not be afraid to experiment: a row of alpine auriculas (*Primula auricula*) are ideal for a small window-box, and a strawberry pot can be planted with small alpine flowers.

Bedding plants provide wonderful splashes of colour just when you need it, when the weather begins to warm up and you want to be out of doors. You can raise your own from seed. Sow most annuals under glass or indoors in early spring and gradually harden them off in a sheltered

Annuals for instant effect

There are two kinds of annuals that you will find on sale in spring. Hardy annuals are those which you can sow easily in window-boxes or tubs (even putting in the seed in autumn, to give it a flying start the following year). Half-hardy annuals are more delicate and have to be raised under glass.

Hardy annuals respond to being grown in tubs and pots, whereas they are likely to get lost in a garden bed or accidentally weeded out at the seedling stage. Plants like pot marigold (*Calendula officinalis*),

place outdoors before finally putting them into their permanent planting as the weather improves. If you prefer it, you can also buy them ready grown, and this is especially useful if growing space is at a premium. It makes sense, in a small space, to start with a backdrop of permanent plants, dominated by evergreens such as rhododendrons or azaleas together with decoratively shaped shrubs or small trees – a dwarf cypress, for instance. With the permanent plants in place you can then give your garden, terrace, or window-box a different look each year by adding colourful annual bedding plants in all their variety.

Petunias and geraniums spilling over a large pot make an eye-catching centre of interest.

cornflowers (*Centaurea cyanus*). *Clarkia*, and *Convolvulus* – all the cottage flowers – can go straight into containers or boxes in March. You can also choose such plants as larkspur (*Delphinium ajacis*), other species of *Delphinium*, annual chrysanthemums, and starry white baby's breath (*Gypsophila*).

The annual sunflower (*Helianthus annuus*), which can grow to 2.5 m (8 ft) makes a cheerful garden screen. If you feel that such height is too great, however, look for the variety 'Dwarf Sungold', which barely reaches 1 m (3 ft). Candytuft (*Iberis*), love-in-a-mist (*Nigella damascena*), poppies (*Papaver*), and phlox will all combine to

give you a country look in a tub, with nasturtiums (*Tropaeolum majus*) trailing over the side. Sow the seed on a warm day and put some fine chicken wire over the area to discourage cats and birds. Or, better still, place a cloche over them to give them a good start. You can also buy, by the metre or yard, plastic reinforced with wire mesh, which can be bent to make tunnel-shaped cloches; you will need wire cutters to cut it into the lengths you require.

Half-hardy annuals have to be raised under glass or indoors to be sure of success. These are the bedding plants that you usually see on sale in street markets, garden

bought in either a compact or a trailing version. Fibrous-rooted begonias are another good choice for a window-box since they go on producing flowers well into late autumn. The tobacco plant (*Nicotiana*), planted in a pot on a sunny window-sill, will reward you with scent in the evening, as will night-scented stock (*Matthiola bicornis*). For more colour impact, cinerarias (*Senecio*), often sold as indoor plants, can be put into window-boxes in summer, although their colours come up best if they are kept away from direct sunlight. Flame nettles (*Coleus*), which are also considered to be indoor plants, have brilliant foliage in reds and

centres, and florists, and they are the mainstay of an instant colourful garden.

For sheer explosive colour you cannot beat petunias (which come in almost every colour from snow white to deep purple), fire-engine-red salvias, and geraniums (properly called pelargoniums – the true geraniums are the perennial crane's-bills). Choose an ivy-leaved variety of geranium if you want trailers or low-growing plants; the others tend to become straggly and ugly by the end of the season. All these flowers will bloom better if you dead-head them.

To complement them you can choose lobelia, another half-hardy which can be

yellows and will happily spend the summer indoors or out.

Biennials (plants which are sown one year and flower the next) that deserve a place on a patio or in a border include that old favourite the wallflower (*Cheiranthus*). Then there is honesty (*Lunaria*), which gives you silvery, paper-like seed-heads for dried-flower arrangements in winter, and the forget-me-not (*Myosotis*). Pansies (*Viola*), strictly speaking perennials, provide pretty, low-growing colour, too. Most biennials will re-seed themselves, so having once installed them you should have fresh plants year after year.

Small-scale colour is best for small, decorative window troughs like these. The *Viola* hybrids are an excellent choice for this kind of situation.

When you are planning for quick colour remember that a small plot in one colour theme looks larger and better planned than a hotch-potch, so it is best to stick to pinks with blues or oranges with reds for a more co-ordinated look. On the other hand, if you are creating a 'cottage-garden look', you can use a wide variety of colours.

Many popular annuals come in several different forms. The pot marigold, for instance, can be found in a dwarf form, 'Baby Gold', which does not need staking. African marigolds (*Tagetes erecta*) make a patch of instant sunshine with their large, orange, pom-pon heads and again range from dwarf to giant forms. African marigolds are half-hardy and should be started off indoors. Cornflowers (*Centaurea*) are usually seen in bright blue but also come in pinks and whites; and love-in-a-mist (*Nigella*) can be found in pink and white as well as the usual dark mauve-blue. There are all sorts of new varieties of low-growing nasturtiums (*Tropaeolum majus*), some of them with double blooms. Look for the compact 'Dwarf Jewel' if you do not want the plants to spread too far. Poppies also come in several different forms, The Iceland poppy (*Papaver nudicaule*), which is grown as a half-hardy annual, has flowers ranging from pink to white and yellow.

When planting bedding plants, carefully tip them out of their pots or boxes (gently squeeze a plastic pot in your hands to loosen a plant, root ball and all). If they have been grown together in a box, carefully separate the plants from each other, leaving as much soil as possible around their roots. Do not leave them lying about while you choose a site; you should have dug holes for them first. In the spring, when you are likely to be putting them in, the weather can be hazardous and their roots could be dried by biting winds. Do not plant bedding plants out in full sunshine, either; wait until the sun has gone down, otherwise they may wilt and die. Water them well and keep an eye on them for a day or so until they are properly established. Do not crowd them too much; they need space to develop.

Backgrounds and bases

Colour in boxes and beds can be heightened and given a more glamorous look if you interplant them with silver-leaved plants. Silver-white colourings, such as those of *Senecio*, also help to make a small plot look larger. *Senecio bicolor* (syn. *S. cineraria*) has very attractive silvery leaves that go well in a window-box; its cultivar 'Silver Dust' is a perennial plant which is

usually treated as a half-hardy annual, although it will often survive a winter out of doors. The shrubby *S. greyi* will give you silvery-grey foliage, and silvery-grey-leaved plants have another bonus – they tend to survive drought better than do green plants as most of them have a protective down on their leaves. Lamb's ears (*Stachys lanata*) mixes well with senecios, and the delicate silver stems of *Artemisia splendens* blend in nicely, too. If you feel you would like a silver corner in the garden or on the edge of a patio, plant the spindle tree, *Euonymus fortunei* 'Silver Queen', which has leaves edged with white. Another variety of this plant, *E. fortunei* 'Colorata', makes good winter ground cover. In a large silvery planting, try adding just one splash of colour to create a focal point. A few poppies would look splendid.

Perennials for colour

Flowering perennials for a permanent flower bed, including most of the plants that make up the traditional herbaceous border, need putting in in the autumn to establish themselves properly for flowering next year. Some perennials may make a glorious display in summer but are less attractive at other times of the year, and if you have a very small plot, it is important to bear this in mind. The best solution is to grow them in tubs, so that they can be moved to a less obtrusive place when their flowering season is over. The red-hot poker (*Kniphofia*) makes a marvellous show in a tall bed, as do arum lilies, and there are lots of daisy-like flowers to choose from: coneflowers (*Rudbeckia*), Michaelmas daisies (*Aster*), which can be chosen in varieties ranging from the very tall to a dwarf version which grows only 150 mm (6 in) high, and marguerites (*Felicia*).

Then there are perennials like the paeony (*Paeonia*), which comes up year after year. Remember that true geraniums (crane's-bills) are half-hardy perennial plants that must be brought in during the winter months. Where space is at a premium it is a good idea to take cuttings from plants in July. Geraniums are just about the easiest plants of all to propagate. Just take off shoots, dip them in hormone rooting powder, and pop them into sandy compost. This will give you new plants for the following year.

Flowering shrubs add their share of colour, too, and require far less work around the patio. Once established they will withstand days without watering, and although they represent a fairly high initial financial outlay, they should be regarded as

The 'cottage-garden' look against a wall: wallflowers are planted cheek by jowl with tulips, aubrietas, and candytuft, while jew's mallow (*Kerria japonica*) sprawls across the background.

a long-term investment. Shrubs will flower year after year without much attention.

Rhododendrons and azaleas provide a wide colour range of attractive blooms and most varieties are evergreen. *Deutzia × elegantissima* is easy to grow and has pretty pink flowers in early summer. The outdoor, hardy fuchsia *F. magellanica*, with its red and blue flowers, makes a good tub specimen, or it will grow to form a mini-hedge around a patio in a warm, sheltered place. There is also a hardy form of hibiscus, *H. syriacus*, which flowers on into the autumn and gives an exotic touch; 'Woodbridge' is a cultivar with deep-pink flowers; 'Mauve Queen' has, as its name implies, mauve flowers, with dark purplish centres. Rock roses (*Cistus*) look very exotic, too; their flowers contain features of both wild rose and hibiscus blooms.

To contrast with flowers like these, the potentillas offer smaller blooms in various colours from reds through to yellows and orange. Blue hydrangeas grown in peaty soil in a tub look good in a corner. Keep them blue by watering them with a special compound you can buy from any garden centre. Not all hydrangeas have large flower-heads; there are 'lacecap' varieties, which have prettier, more complicated, delicate flowers in the centre – look for the names 'Blue Wave' and 'White Wave'.

There are several dwarf shrubs that seldom grow more than 300 mm (12 in) high. *Berberis corallina compacta*, for instance, has coral-red buds followed by golden flowers. *Hebe darwiniana* has pretty grey foliage, and the tiny *Rhododendron impeditum* grows scarcely more than 450 mm (18 in) high and has blue-violet flowers.

Roses

Roses give a show of colour throughout the summer that is virtually unequalled by any other shrub. Hybrid tea roses are the cheapest, most easily found varieties – you can often find them on sale in supermarkets, for instance. But in some cases scent has been sacrificed for colour and shape. So, to get the most out of your roses in a small space, pick varieties that have perfume as well as colour – for instance, 'Fragrant Cloud', a red rose that has a heavy scent. Hybrid tea roses should flower from June to October if you dead-head them regularly, and they will stand anything but full shade. However, they are prone to diseases like black spot and mildew, so they need careful watching and prompt action with the relevant fungicides to avoid becoming sickly plants. Most hybrid tea roses will

Permanent plantings and container plants are mixed to great effect in this small London garden, where a potted begonia is the central feature of a mini-parterre made of box (*Buxus*); and red geraniums (*Pelargonium*) stand like guardsmen in the background.

grow happily in containers, as long as you feed them with a fertilizer such as bone meal. Where there is a little more space available, shrub roses give a 'country' look in a town setting. Some of them have very simple flowers, almost like wild roses – for example, *Rosa gallica* 'Complicata' and *Rosa* 'Ballerina', a hybrid musk.

Most old roses of this kind need plenty of space in which to grow and have a shorter flowering season than the more modern varieties. But if you choose one of the dwarf polyanthas, such as 'Paul Crampel' (with orange red flowers) or 'Perle d'Or' (with yellow blooms), they do not grow much

more than 600 mm (2 ft) high and usually flower twice in a season, once in early summer and again in September.

Where space is very limited, on a window-sill, for instance, miniature roses come into their own. But they need to be sited at about waist level to be seen properly. In addition to taking up very little space they are, on the whole, less thorny than conventional roses – an advantage in a small space. Miniature roses prefer to be grown by themselves, rather than grouped with other plants , so it is preferable to keep each in a pot, either as a specimen plant or, with the pot plunged into the soil of a window-box, as part of a display. Their requirements are exactly the same as those of conventional roses. If miniature roses are kept indoors all summer they will almost certainly die, for they need a great deal of light. They can, however, be brought in for, say, a week at a time to provide spot colour when it is needed. These small roses tend to be rather more prone to disease than the larger varieties, so keep a special eye on them. They grow best in John Innes No 1 compost (the one usually used for seedlings); re-pot them each year and give them a mulch of peat in the winter.

Some good miniature roses to look out for include 'Baby Gold Star', which will grow to just over 300 mm (12 in) tall and has yellow semi-double flowers; 'Cinderella', a very pretty pink-white rose which reaches only about 225 mm (9 in) high; 'Pixie', which has double pink flowers; and 'Perla de Alcanada', which has semi-double deep carmine flowers. There are also several climbing miniature roses which are very pretty on a balcony or in a window-box. 'Magic Wand' has bright red flowers with white centres; 'Show-off', has beige flowers with orange markings; the best known, 'Pink Cameo', can sometimes be seen as a weeping standard rose in a pot on a terrace. Miniature roses are sometimes difficult to track down, so it is well worthwhile finding a specialist nursery for these.

A modern climbing rose, 'Étude', gives a countrified look in a town setting. Although vigorous in growth it makes a good rose for a modest garden as it rarely exceeds 2.4m (8ft).

Colourful foliage

Foliage makes almost as much impact as do flowers in bringing contrast and sometimes colour instantly to a small area. For free-standing greenery in a very small space you can use bonsai trees. These are artificially dwarfed shrubs and trees which many people mistakenly believe need to be grown indoors. They are, in fact, outdoor plants and make a very striking impact in terms of shape on a small patio or a window-sill. While a true bonsai tree takes years to

grow to its proper form, most small varieties of trees that shed their leaves can be miniaturized to some extent. To miniaturize a tree, keep it in a smaller pot than it would normally be given. In early spring cut off half of each leaf with sharp scissors on the weaker branches and remove the leaves completely from the stronger ones. After a while the leaf stalks will drop off and new smaller foliage will grow. This type of rather drastic pruning can be done only on trees that do not produce flowers or fruit. The Japanese maple *Acer palmatum* 'Atropurpureum', whose leaves turn a deep scarlet-purple, makes a very good

specimen tree to grow in a half-barrel or tub.

The stripy, ribbed leaves of the giant plantain lilies (*Hosta*) look splendid in tubs or planted under a small tree, as do the pale green flowers of stinking hellebore (*Helleborus foetidus*), which look almost like leaves. And it is here that herbs, too, come into their own, not only providing flavour in the kitchen but also colour in the garden. Rue (*Ruta gravcolens*) has very attractive blue-green foliage and delicate leaves; choose the variety 'Jackman's Blue' for the best effect. Set against that there is the fresh yellowy, almost spring green of feverfew (*Tanacetum parthenium*) and the deep lush

The variegated leaves of the plantain lily *Hosta fortunei* 'Albopicta' make an attractive sea of greenery; here they provide an excellent foil for colourful primulas.

green of parsley (*Petroselinum crispum*), which makes a marvellous mini-border or edging for a tub. Golden thyme (*Thymus vulgaris*) and golden marjoram (*Origanum vulgare* 'Aureum') both look good either mixed with silver foliage or on their own. Rosemary (*Rosmarinus officinalis*) has attractive needle-like leaves and pretty blue flowers. Borage (*Borago officinalis*), even if it does tend to become untidy, has pretty, blue, star-like flowers that go well in summer salads and drinks. It self-seeds itself ready for next year and attracts bees too. The striking foliage of lovage (*Levisticum officinale*), whose leaves taste and smell strongly of celery and can be used as a substitute for it in salads, looks good in small garden plantings. So does angelica (*Angelica archangelica*), but do not let it form seed heads if you want to keep it from one year to the next. The feathery foliage of fennel (*Foeniculum vulgare*) and dill (*Peucedanum graveolens*) look good with the silver of sage (*Salvia officinalis*).

Fruit and vegetables can contribute to colour in a window-box as well as in the garden proper. The salad tomato 'Tiny Tim', for instance, grows in a bushy form and is perfectly happy in a window-box. It bears dozens of cherry-sized tomatoes, which look very pretty indeed. The lettuce 'Tom Thumb', which can be easily grown from seed, makes an attractive light green edging if you prick out the seedlings around the edge of a tub containing a small specimen tree. Salad-bowl lettuce can also be grown in this way. In larger areas globe artichokes form magnificent blue, thistle-like heads – although if you let them flower you lose the artichokes, which are, in fact, the buds. Runner beans, which come in varieties with white, salmon pink, or red flowers, add to colour in the garden before they produce their very welcome vegetable bonus. There is also a carrot variety that grows in a window-box, producing green ferny foliage as well as carrots to eat.

Winter colour

It is a pity that many people leave their window-boxes and tubs bare in winter, just when they are needed most to provide interest and colour. Even if a window-box contains only a mini-hedge of green, it is more attractive to look at than an empty box or a bare window-sill. There are plenty of dwarf evergreens that make a good backdrop for both spring bulbs and bedding-out plants in summer. Look out for dwarf conifers which are available in columnar or round shapes. Box (*Buxus*) is a

very accommodating background evergreen, and its tiny leaves can be clipped to make a neat edge to a box or tub. If you are short of space, these evergreens can be carefully moved to a quiet corner of the garden to spend the summer months.

Do not discount variegated ivies (*Hedera*) for all-year-round colour. For larger tubs you may like to choose holly (*Ilex*): you can buy it container-grown in the autumn with its berries on, ready for a winter show. *I. aquifolium* 'Pyramidalis' or, if you want a dwarf form, Japanese holly (*I. crenata*) 'Mariesii' are good varieties to choose. Berries play an important part in

winter colour. *Skimmia japonica* 'Foremanii' has bright orange-red berries that last all winter, and the flowering crab apple (*Malus*) 'Evereste' keeps its bright red crab apples on until spring and grows happily in a tub.

There is an enormous variety of small trees and shrubs that can be container-grown to give you colour in winter, a time when it is much needed. Forsythias, for instance, have starry yellow flowers that sometimes arrive with the snow. *Mahonia japonica*, which has yellow flowers that smell rather like lily-of-the-valley, also blooms early in the year. Winter jasmine (*Jasminum nudiflorum*) flowers from mid-autumn to early spring. There are also winter-flowering rhododendrons that can be container grown; one, appropriately named 'Christmas Cheer', has pretty pink flowers, while 'Praecox' has lilac-purple blooms. The Chinese azalea (*Rhododendron simsii*) can be brought indoors as a pot plant in the autumn, when it should flower during the winter months in the house.

Bulbs and corms play an important part in the winter garden, whether they are in a box or around the edge of a courtyard. Snowdrops and crocuses, swiftly followed by the first daffodils, make all the difference in a small plot. If space is very limited, plant

There is no need to leave your window-box bare of plants in winter. This one is furnished all the year round with miniature conifers and ivy. The begonias can be replaced by bulbs to provide colour in the winter.

the 'species' bulbs, which are smaller and simpler. They are, in fact, the original versions of irises, daffodils, and tulips and they look good growing in a pot or in a small window-box. *Narcissus minimus*, for instance, grows only 75 mm (3 in) tall; the lady tulip (*Tulipa clusiana*) reaches about 150 mm (6 in), and the tiny *Iris histrioides* is hard put to exceed 100 mm (4 in) in height.

I. histrioides 'Major', which is a deep blue marked with gold, and *I. reticulata*, violet coloured and sweetly scented, look good in tubs or boxes or in a quiet corner of a backyard garden; they flower in the first months of the year. Small cyclamens, such as *Cyclamen ibericum*, bloom from January until March if planted in the autumn.

The hellebores are also winter-flowering plants and you could try growing the Christmas rose (*Helleborus niger*) in really rich compost. It needs plenty of fertilizer in the summer months if it is to survive and you must be careful to see that it does not dry out. In the late autumn, when the first signs of flower buds appear, cover the plant with a piece of a cloche or tent of clear plastic (use a hoop of wire to make sure the plastic does not touch the plant); this will gently 'force' the flowers.

Even a hanging basket can be a blaze of flowers in winter if you plant it with winter-flowering pansies (*Viola*) such as 'Azure Blue' and 'Golden Sunny Boy', while heathers (*Erica*) look good in an architectural setting such as a patio or a paved courtyard. Winter heath (*Erica carnea*) is the most accommodating of the family, for it will tolerate some lime (most ericas need an acid soil), and it produces masses of pretty pink bells in the winter. Camellias too, which many people shrink from growing because of their reputation for being very choosy, do well in places where they do not suffer extremes of temperature. Surprisingly, a camellia often does best on a north wall, because there it has some protection against frost and early morning sun. Camellias tend to grow slowly, but they need little attention apart from a mulch of peat to protect their roots in winter. *Camellia × williamsii* is not known as the perpetual-flowering camellia for nothing, and will normally bloom from January until April. There are many cultivars, of which 'Charles Michael' (single pink flowers), 'Caerhays' (bright mauve-pink, semi-double flowers), and 'Francis Hanger' (single white blooms) are among the best.

In a large tub the flowering cherry (*Prunus subhirtella cantabrigiensis*) makes a marvellous show with some of the earliest blossom in the year.

Winter aconite (*Eranthus hyemalis*) provides a welcome splash of colour right at the beginning of the year. It is easily grown and will happily partner snowdrops or crocuses.

THE OUTDOOR ROOM

You can think of a large balcony, terrace, or patio as an outdoor room, even if the walls are invisible. If you want privacy, then defining these walls in some way can make a tremendous difference to the atmosphere of the area when you are sitting out. Even a 'skeleton' of wooden pots, trellis, or netting can create at least the illusion that you are not overlooked.

In cramped city conditions a 'ceiling' of laths or planks (suspended on edge) with creepers growing over them can block out the upstairs neighbours' view of you and give you the feeling that you are in your own outdoor dining room. If you want to, you can add clear corrugated PVC sheeting on top, which will shut out the worst of the weather (though raindrops can make a fearful clatter on PVC) and act as a greenhouse over the climbers beneath. Any such roofing, incidentally, should have a slight slope so that the rain runs off it. You can also use the space under the planks to suspend plantpots and hanging baskets.

An indoor/outdoor link

There are several ways in which you can form a link between your house and your outdoor room in order to create an outdoor atmosphere indoors. For example, you can grow the same climber immediately inside and outside a window; you could choose a variegated ivy and have one plant growing in a pot just inside the window and another climbing up the wall outside. Make sure, too, that the window nearest to the balcony or patio has plenty of plants growing in pots on its sill, to give a garden feel to that part of the room.

Another way to get that indoor/outdoor link is with colour. You can match up the colour of a painted indoor wall or just one colour in the wallpaper with the flowers outside. A room with yellow curtains could be matched by yellow flowers out on the patio. A tub of bright tulips outside will immediately lead the eye beyond the room if they tune in with the wall. Red is a particularly striking colour when used in this way. For example, you could have scarlet geraniums in a flower bed or pot picking up the red in a wallpaper pattern.

Paving

If you have a sitting-out area in your back yard or courtyard, then it is a good idea to define it in some way. You could, for instance, set it apart from the rest of the area by paving it. An area of paving slabs will raise the ground level very slightly (but not

enough to be a nuisance) and give you somewhere definite to sit. The process of defining your area could then be taken a stage further by having narrow troughs of box (*Buxus*) or other evergreens around the edge of the paving to make a miniature free-standing hedge. Another idea that works well is to build a low cavity wall – two rows of bricks with a gap of about 100 mm (4 in) between them, tied together by brickwork at both ends. The gap is then filled with soil in which dwarf plants or alpines can be grown. Another way of having plants alongside the patio is to build a low wall, missing out a brick here and there and putting in soil instead. The gaps can then be planted with alpines. It is a good idea to incorporate strips of chicken wire into the gaps which will help keep the soil in place.

In an existing patio that is nothing more than a smooth concrete platform, an area of interest can be made by laying a 'carpet' of ceramic tiles in the centre. This is cheaper than covering the whole area and is just as effective. You can then pick up the colours in the tiles with flowers around the side. Some of the same tiles could also be fixed in a band on the house wall, between shelving or boxes of plants, to link it visually with the floor for additional effect.

There is an enormous selection of paving available now. Real York stone is very expensive, but it is ideal if you want a weathered country-house look or if you are matching paving with a period property. Local councils seldom seem to have second-hand paving stones to spare, nowadays, but if you can get hold of them they are very attractive, since they are already worn. They are larger than the standard sizes, which is often an advantage. Precast concrete paving is now much better than it used to be and comes with various types of non-slip surfaces and in muted colours. You may like to achieve a two-tone effect by using two different shades of paving stone alternately. This is less monotonous than one shade if you have a large area to cover.

Paving stones are easy enough to lay provided you have a reasonable surface underneath. They can be placed on existing concrete without using cement, if the concrete surface is absolutely clean and level. If you are starting from scratch, it may be necessary to begin with a layer of hardcore followed by a layer of sand to obtain the desired level before the slabs are laid. Always remember to have a slight slope – about 25 mm per 2 m (1 in per 6 ft) will do – so that the rain will run off rather than lie around in puddles on the patio. In a roof garden or balcony, where pre-cast

Page 90 Plants to create a two-way effect: the greenery of the pots, tubs, and hanging baskets leads the eye out into the garden and brings the garden into the home.

Plants grouped both
inside and outside a
window have a softening
effect and attractively blur
the boundary between
house and garden. The
effect is even stronger if
the same species is used
inside and out.

paving would probably be too heavy, lighter-weight paving bricks and quarry tiles may be a better choice.

Another, cheaper way to lay a patio is to concrete it. You can cut the concrete into squares to simulate paving stones while it is still damp. Mark out the squares beforehand by making marks on the side of the house and hammering sticks into the ground opposite them. Then use a plank, held sideways on, to make a deep cut in the concrete, making sure that it does not go quite all the way down to the sand beneath. If you have a large area to cover, it pays to make up a squared framework of battens and put it down before you pour the concrete. Lift out the framework once the mix has begun to dry and has shrunk slightly. Whatever type of paving you choose, remember that it should be easy to clean.

For a really comfortable sitting-out area that will take a table seating four people, you need a depth of at least 2.5 m (8 ft) and as much length as is available. Your patio should, if possible, be sited where it will catch most of the sun. But if it is going to be used mainly on summer evenings, you will probably want to ensure that it catches the evening sun. And if you are going to use it for entertaining and serving food, then you may want to have at least some shade. Generally, it is best to put your seating near the house for maximum shelter and convenience; in the typical small town garden, of course, you will not have a choice in the matter.

Pergolas

A network of posts, known as a pergola, over a patio makes all the difference in terms of the illusion of privacy, especially if you have plenty of cross-pieces overhead. If it is possible to tie these into the house walls for extra strength and rigidity, so much the better. Ideally, oak or cedar is used for pergola poles, but both are extremely expensive and most people use the cheaper larch or pine instead. Remember to treat all timbers with some form of preservative before you nail or screw them in place. The uprights must be well bedded into the ground, preferably in concrete to a depth of at least 450 mm (18 in). Alternatively, they can be set into the patio when it is being constructed, or put into sockets (pieces of soil pipe will do) which are set into concrete. Remember that they will have to take quite heavy loads. High winds, particularly in roof gardens, heavy climbers dragging at them, and, occasionally, high spirited people

The clever distribution of plants in large containers in this inner courtyard shows just how much greenery, including even small trees, you can get into a small space without overcrowding.

swinging on them, can all take their toll of pergola poles. As an alternative to sawn timber, you can use the rustic poles that are sold by most garden centres. Do-it-yourself pergola kits, complete with precision-cut components that can be fixed easily together are also available. On a smaller scale – on a balcony, for instance – you can get a similar effect by standing lightweight poles in tubs and growing climbers such as passion flowers (*Passiflora caerulea*) up them. Another solution is to build a network of canes overhead and on each side of the balcony.

Outdoor lights

Lighting, if it is skilfully used, can turn a patio or a balcony into something like a stage set at the touch of a switch. Spotlights, for instance, can be fixed to the walls or pergola poles to highlight particular plants in the way that one would highlight a precious painting. A statue, too, looks very dramatic when lit at night, and anything with striking foliage will look even more attractive when treated this way. Alternatively, the whole area can be floodlit; in a small space one tungsten lamp will turn it into another room. You can also buy pool lights that will create yet another dimension, highlighting and changing the colour of the water and altering the character of the whole area.

With lighting you can draw attention to the things that you want people to see, such as attractive plants, and leave items such as dustbins in the darkness. You can buy spotlights on spikes which you stick into the ground or into pots, and you can move them around at will. They are best placed as low as possible for the greatest possible effect. Lights do not necessarily have to be only for summer use. A snow-covered backyard can be made to look like a living Christmas card scene when flood lights are switched on to it. More practically, lighting is also a deterrent to burglars.

Candles in barbecue lanterns or jamjars can make attractive temporary lighting if you are eating out. Lights, unfortunately, always attract insects, but you can now buy special electric patio lanterns which not only provide light but also kill insects that come near them. There are also infra-red heaters that can be used out of doors to provide warmth.

Whatever lighting you use it is essential to have its installation done by a professional. Unprotected cables and indoor sockets and plugs simply will not do outside; they are dangerous. Waterproof plugs are essential and all equipment must be properly earthed and installed. The best and safest garden lighting is the type in which power is taken from the mains but is stepped down, via a transformer, to a much less dangerous 12 volts.

Plants for an outdoor room

Vines, whether you choose the traditional grape vine (*Vitis vinifera*) or the Russian vine (*Polygonum baldschuanicum*), make the best climbers to scramble up the posts of a pergola if it borders a sitting-out area. Clematis tends to be rather delicate for the job; and roses, which are often traditionally grown this way, can be tiresome in a confined space, as their thorns catch on clothing and scratch. If you want to have a rose, choose a thorn-free variety or put it against a back wall.

Bear in mind if you are planting climbers that lanterns, if you use them, will tend to burn their foliage. If you are planning a barbecue, even a free-standing one, keep the site free from permanent plants; instead, use tub-grown specimens that can be moved away from any flames.

Hanging baskets look delightful dangling from the cross-pieces of a pergola and are particularly useful during the time when young climbers are growing. If you use them in this way you will need to stock them with trailing plants, since they will be seen mainly from underneath.

If planting around the bases of poles is a problem, it is possible to grow climbers in containers set above, on the joints of the cross-pieces, and let them trail down. But such containers must be properly secured; plastic cones can be fixed with nuts, bolts, and washers, and wooden ones can be screwed into place. Remember, too, that you can fix potted plants in holders on the posts, where they will grow happily. This is an attractive way to use that brief-flowering annual climber morning glory (*Ipomoea*), with its scarlet or purple blooms.

There is a huge variety of garden furniture to be found, ranging from exotic cane chairs to rustic tables and benches. In a confined space, however, it is not only the appearance of the furniture that counts but also what you can do with it on a long-term basis. Some items, for instance, can be left outside all year round; others cannot and you have to find somewhere to store them.

Cast-iron of cast-aluminium Victorian-style chairs and tables will withstand the weather provided you keep them painted. They look very attractive standing outside, actively contributing to the attractive

A well-established grape-vine growing overhead has helped to turn this area into an attractive garden room. A similar effect could be achieved in just a few years with a quick-growing climber such as Russian vine.

appearance of the garden or balcony. However, their great disadvantage is that they are very heavy. They are also usually rather uncomfortable to sit on, although cushions can remedy that problem. 'Victorian' designs are also available in lightweight white plastic. Metal furniture that is comfortable to sit on can be rather unattractive to look at, but it is worth watching out for new designs.

Bamboo, rush, and basket furniture is very pleasant to relax in, but it usually takes up a great deal of space. It cannot be left out of doors for long as it will rot, and it tends to attract insects and mildew. But if you have the space to bring it indoors during the winter months – basket chairs are often useful and attractive in bedrooms – it can be the ideal garden furniture. Wooden furniture will last longer than basketware and can be attractive in a country-style backyard or a roof garden; but it, too, tends to be large and get in the way, and seldom looks right on a balcony or small patio.

It pays to look around the junk shops for unusual items of furniture for the patio. The base of an old treadle sewing machine, given a new wooden top or, better still, a marble one from a washstand, makes a very attractive small patio table. A space-saver in a really small back yard is a garden hammock to relax in, slung between two posts or two trees. And if you are really stuck for space in a yard or a balcony, consider large floor cushions or blow-up plastic airbeds. Alternatively, go for fold-up chairs – 'film director' chairs are attractive and can also be used indoors as extra seating. Stackable stools also take up little space. If you are using cushions on seating, wipe-clean plastic ones are not very pleasant to sit on. It is better to choose fabric cushions and either store them in large plastic (waterproof) bags or take them indoors when they are not in use.

If dining space is limited, you could incorporate a snack bar into the top of a low brick wall, putting a table top on it, or have a table top that hinges against the wall of the house. This can also work on a balcony.

Barbecues are great fun, and where space is short it is best to buy a self-contained one. If you can find a spare corner, however, it is easy to make a barbecue with bricks. Build three sides of a rectangle up to the required height and fit a wire tray and a grid (an old oven shelf is ideal for this) into the top courses. Always site a barbecue well away from anything inflammable, such as a wooden fence or pole: flames go a surprisingly long way on a windy night and sparks fly, too.

A large conservatory can become an exciting place to eat all the year round if it is turned into a mini-jungle. Daylight filtering through the green makes it look good by day; at night floodlighting creates even more dramatic effects.

Mirrors to 'stretch' your patio

It pays to think of every trick you can to stretch space in an outdoor room. Making an area seem twice the size it really is can be achieved most easily with mirrors, provided you have a solid wall to attach them to.

Two mirrors placed facing one another on the end walls of a balcony will reflect images from one to the other and the result is an apparently never-ending space. Plant some climbers to hide their edges, create a focal point such as a small fountain or a statue between them, and the result can be delightful. The same effect can be achieved in a back yard, of course, but at far greater cost as you will need very large mirrors. On a much smaller scale, however, a mirror fixed to the wall with creepers round it to hide the edges, or with trellis placed just in front of it, gives the impression that you are looking through a window into another part of the garden. You can even put a window frame over it to make it more realistic.

If you can lay your hands on a really large mirror – from an old wardrobe door, for instance – you can have a great deal of fun by putting a wrought-iron gate immediately in front of it. On the other hand you could build a trellis arch, or better still a brick one, around it. To make the effect believable, however, the edges must always be concealed in some way with battening or false architraves, otherwise they give the game away. You can now buy glass-fibre reproductions of Georgian pediments and columns, and these can look very attractive flanking a mirror in a 'period' courtyard.

Whichever way you use it, the mirror must have a waterproof backing. If you are in any doubt, make sure that the edges are sealed off effectively and, to be on the safe side, use a stick-on plastic covering on the back to protect it from water. A mirror must be angled very carefully, and it is a two-man job to fix it in place. Unless you are careful it will reflect only the sky or the ground or perhaps an unattractive aspects of the plot. It should be angled very slightly, so that it does not reflect *you* directly when you are standing opposite that part of the wall.

A good, cheaper substitute for a mirror in a place that is protected from the rain is metalised plastic, which can be bought by the metre in shops that specialise in decorative display papers. If you choose the heaviest weight (400 g/m²), which is flexible but fairly stiff, it can be stapled on to a piece of marine ply with a staple gun, or simply nailed in place using large-headed tacks or drawing pins. It is difficult to get this

Mirrors are magic space-stretchers in a confined area. Here one is placed behind a yucca, with trelliswork around it to distort the perspective.

Opposite page In this delightful stencil fantasy a formal fruit-bearing tree has 'grown' out of a drainpipe trunk. A simple design like this could be drawn by anyone.

Below If you have no space for flowers, paint your own! This street-facing wall is boldly decorated from pavement to eaves with larger than life-size blooms.

sheeting absolutely smooth, but the distorted images it produces can be great fun. Mirrors and mirror-like materials are particularly effective if you place a half basket in front of them well planted with colourful flowers. You can put a mirror behind a semi-circular pool; this will create the illusion that the pond is, in fact, circular.

You will need plastic wall fixings and brass screws to fix a mirror in place out of doors. Put thick rubber washers between the mirror and the wall to make sure that it does not crack when you tighten it up. Remember that glass expands in high temperatures and contracts in sub-zero ones, so do not screw it in place too tightly.

Creating illusions

The art of using trellis to deceive the eye has been used for centuries and it makes good sense in a small area. On a wall that is already covered by trellis, it is a good idea to set aside a space for a fake arch. Choose an area about the size of a doorway and decide on a 'vanishing point', as if you were drawing in perspective at eye level. Mark this with a piece of chalk, then surround the area with an arch, which can either be made

out of steamed and bent batten or cut out of plywood with a jigsaw. Now cut and fit a series of trellis battens around the arch, making sure that if they were continued through it to the centre they would touch the chalk mark. Fix the top battens first, one each side of the centre, then go out from there. The ones at eye level (that is, the level of the 'vanishing point') should be parallel to the ground. Remember that the more sharply they slope, the deeper the archway will look. To finish the effect, add another arch at their outer edges. If you paint the centre of the arch a dark colour or, better still, fill it in with mirror, the effect is even more striking.

There are many other ways to deceive the eye. A door fixed to the wall makes everyone think that it leads somewhere. A wall painted in two colours – light coloured 'arches' over a dark ground – can give the impression that beyond it is a covered walk. You can take this a stage further by using columns made from plastic drain piping, topped by marine ply with arches cut into it, fixed to the wall.

A wall that is painted white seems to be larger than it actually is; and the garden therefore seems more spacious. Flowers

planted in front of such a wall seem lighter and brighter too; even plain green takes on a chic look. You could hire an artist, of course, to paint a realistic scene on a wall, but it is more fun to try to do it yourself. A Rousseauesque jungle, for instance, can be painted quite easily, using the leaves of real plants to cut stencils. Or you can paint the foliage of, say, a yucca or a fern on a wall then put the real thing in front to give a three-dimensional effect.

Plants can also be used to deceive the eye. Certain conifers, for instance, which we are used to seeing in their normal size can be bought in dwarf forms as well. So if you plant a really small-scale conifer at the end of a courtyard or on the edge of a balcony, the eye assumes that it is farther away than it actually is, provided that everything else is in scale. Darker shades of green seem farther away than lighter ones. A curved line seems longer than a straight line, for the eye takes longer to follow it. You can play further tricks by having a straight path that narrows to meet a small fake trellis archway, deluding the onlooker into thinking that the latter is a long way away.

Ponds and pools

Water adds another dimension to patio living. Because it reflects the sky, it makes a courtyard seem more spacious. The gentle splash of a fountain is very pleasant to hear on a patio or a balcony, where you can easily have a free-standing pond with trailing plants over the side.

Choose a pool to suit your setting. Generally, straight lines in a patio dictate a square or rectangular pond. It is a good idea to incorporate a pond into the patio design, leaving out a square or two of paving, perhaps, or building a brick container to hold it above ground level. The irregular outlines of the free-form fibreglass pools that can be bought ready-made are usually best used in a rockery setting or cut into a lawn – although that lawn could well be chamomile (*Anthemis nobilis*), since this will grow attractively over the side. Before putting a pool on a balcony or roof garden, however, check on how much water you are likely to need: water weighs 800 g per litre (8 lb per gallon), so a large water-filled container will put a very considerable strain on the structure. Check also that you have a water supply nearby to service it, as a pool will need topping up regularly. It will lose a considerable amount of water through evaporation, especially if it has a fountain, and you will soon tire of carrying buckets of water upstairs.

Water lilies give great pleasure if planted in small pools as specimen blooms. This beautiful *Nymphaea laydekeri* 'Lilacea' flowers freely but needs a water depth of up to 750mm (30in).

Almost anything watertight can be turned into an instant pond. Even a discarded bath can be used so long as you hide its all-too-obvious edges. Old sinks, large basins, and large bowls are also useful in confined spaces. All these containers, even if they are cracked and leaky, make a good basis for a pool, since they can be lined with heavy-duty black polythene.

If you decide to dig your own pond, mark it out first with string and pegs. When you shape the sides, cut them in one or more steps with sloping sides rather than as a single vertical drop; then you can use extra marginal plants, and the walls are less likely to fall in. To calculate the amount of pond liner needed, measure the length and width of the pond and add *twice* the depth to each measurement. For example, if your pool is 600 × 900 mm (2 × 3 ft) and 300 mm (1 ft) deep, you will need a sheet of polythene 1.2 × 1.5 m (4 × 5 ft) in size. Put the polythene in place in warm weather, when it will be more pliable and will cling to the curves, or warm it slightly indoors first. Carefully lay the liner over the hole, weighing it down with a few smooth pebbles in the bottom and on the stepped sides. Then fill it slowly with a hose. When it is full you can smooth the

surplus polythene over the surrounding surface and cover its edges with stone, brick, or concrete coping. If the pool is being made on a terrace, fill it before laying the surrounding paving stones, so that these can be used as coping. You can leave little pockets of soil around the edges and plant pond-side trailing plants.

A plastic garden urn, with its drainage holes blocked, or a free-standing sink are the best pools to use on a balcony, where flooding would be a disaster. Or you could place a bucket inside a more decorative holder, such as a small wooden tub. Plastic plant tubs also make good ponds and will accommodate a fountain. A point to remember, by the way, if you are playing with water at that height is that wind can cause havoc; on blustery days the fountain that you so admire may give your neighbours an unwelcome cold shower.

Small submersible pumps are available in sizes so small they can be used as part of table decorations. They have one snag: despite their filters they tend to clog up, so it is important to keep your pool water as clean as you possibly can. The best way to do this is to instal oxygenating plants, such as water moss (*Fontinalis antipyretica*),

A tiny patio pond creates an interesting focal point in a paved area. If it is custom-built into the patio paving, as here, it will not over-dominate the confined space.

spiked water milfoil (*Myriophyllum spicatum*), which has delicate fine-toothed leaves, and curled pondweed (*Potamogeton crispus*), which looks more like a seaweed than a pond weed.

The stars of the show are the water-lilies. They look very exotic, but they are surprisingly easy to grow. Once they are anchored in place they need little or no attention. The hybrid lily *Nymphaea* 'Aurora', for instance, is good for small pools since it only needs about 225 mm (9 in) of water to grow in; it has deep yellow flowers that darken with age to red. There is a number of lilies that will grow very happily in tub pools; for example, *N. nitida*, which has cup-shaped flowers which appear in early summer, and *N. odorata* 'Sulphurea', which has bright yellow blooms.

Many of the water-lilies are fragrant. *N.* 'Froebelii', for instance, has scented flowers in a deep crimson hue, and *N.* 'Graziella' has attractive red-bronze flowers that gradually fade to orange. If you are planning a really small pond – in a window box for instance – there are two small water-lilies that you can use: *N. pygmaea* 'Alba' has tiny white, scented flowers little more

than 50 mm (2 in) across and will survive in water only 150 mm (6 in) deep; *N. pygmaea* 'Helvola', with star-like yellow blooms, will grow even in a pudding basin or a fish tank (which, incidentally, makes a good window-sill pool). Pygmy lilies in shallow water need bringing indoors in the winter if there is a sharp frosty spell. If the pool cannot be moved, cover the plants with a wooden board in cold weather.

Water lilies should be planted in May or June. They are available from most large garden centres, although you will need to go to a specialist grower if you are looking for anything unusual. A specialist will also give you useful advice on stocking your pool, and help you to resist the temptation to put too many plants in.

Fill your pool and let it warm up before putting plants in. If you are planning to plant a lily on the bottom, shovel in some soil (not peat or leaf-mould, as these will turn sour and float). Add a little charcoal to keep the soil sweet, and if possible lay a piece of turf on top. It will take two or three days for the soil to settle down and the pond to warm up.

Anchor the water lily to the soil in the base of the pond with a pebble or two, or plant it in a purpose-built basket available

Moving water is delightful to hear as well as to look at. This neat pond and fountain reflect the clean, uncluttered lines of their town-house setting.

from an aquatic specialist. Lower the tuber carefully into the water, making sure that when it is in place the crown is only just below the surface. If it is too deep, raise the soil or the basket to the required level, or bale out some water. In time the plant will grow and you can re-adjust the water level.

You can add to your garden pool by surrounding it with plants that appreciate damp conditions, especially if you have a fountain. Bugle (*Ajuga reptans*), with its copper-coloured foliage and blue flower spikes, is a good creeping perennial for this spot. Many of the attractive ferns also appreciate a watery setting, and benefit from the humid atmosphere immediately around the pond. False goat's beard (*Astilbe*), which has feather-like plumes of white, pink, and red with very attractive foliage, also likes a moist position.

Trees and hedges

You can furnish your patio with some attractive standard trees. Many flowering plants can be turned into pot-grown decorative standards with very little trouble if they are started early enough, and many familiar houseplants can also be turned into indoor trees. Examples include geraniums (including scented-leaved varieties) and fuchsias (which make very decorative weeping standards). Then there are marguerites (*Felicia amelloides*), Michaelmas daisies (*Aster novi-belgii*), and other herbaceous plants. Flame nettles (*Coleus*), indoor plants with brightly coloured leaves, make good-looking standards that are better in many ways than the normal shrubby plants. Then there is, of course, the bay tree (*Laurus nobilis*), which is often professionally grown as a standard.

To grow a standard start with a small rooted cutting or strong seedling, the straightest one you can find. Put it in a 100 mm (4 in) pot and tie the stem to a small stake. Allow the side leaves to grow at this stage, but nip out any lateral shoots; these usually appear in the leaf axils (the places where the side leaves join the stem). As the plant grows taller, repot it and restake it. When it reaches the height you require, nip off the growing tip to force the plant to make top branches and to develop a crown. When this has become established, remove the side leaves from the main stem. You will then have a standard tree that you can shape and clip as the seasons go by.

Plants grown as small standard trees will last for many years, given the right care. If you want a weeping tree, such as a fuchsia, tie cotton strands carefully to the tips of the

branches and peg them back into the ground with hairpins or forked sticks. Standards need feeding well and potting on when they outgrow their containers.

Most specimen trees look attractive around a patio or on a balcony; this is often where they can be seen to their best advantage. Look for dwarf versions of anything with a good shape; small cypresses, for instance, take well to tubs and are particularly good in a formal setting.

On a balcony or patio wall you can grow trees on a much smaller scale. A discarded sink makes a splendid small garden to place near eye level for growing miniature conifers and roses. This is also a good way to grow alpines and small-scale 'species' daffodils and tulips, which tend to become lost in larger beds. It is important that such sink gardens have adequate drainage, although in summer they will tend to dry out quickly. Use John Innes No 2 compost for the soil, and do not feed the plants with fertilizer or they will tend to 'bolt' and become too large for their setting.

Finally, patio and balcony topiary is fun, too. There is no reason why you should not have a row of tiny clipped and trained trees along your window-sill. Choose box (*Buxus*) for this purpose. Buy a small, well-grown, bushy plant about 150 mm (6 in) high, and train it to the shape you require. You can either clip it into a simple shape, such as a cone, sphere, or cube, using kitchen scissors to trim the plant regularly as it grows taller and bushes out; or, if you have a slender plant with only one main stem, you can put a stake in the pot and twist the stem around it, tying it at intervals with string, so that it grows into a spiral.

To make your own topiary animals or birds, take a good look at the plant to assess its potential. If, for example, its shape reminds you of a swan, take some stout wire and bend it roughly into the shape of the subject. For a bird you would loop the wire into two ovals, one for the head and another larger one for the body, with the end bent up for a tail. Entwine the wire firmly into the main stem of the plant just where it begins to make shoots, then train the growing shoots round the wire, covering as much of it as possible to build up the outline. Do not clip the plant at this stage, but trim it lightly as it gradually takes shape. Birds are probably the easiest shapes to tackle; other animals may need as many as four plants in a row – one for each foot.

Another form of topiary is to make a shape in the form of a wire frame and then to train small-leaved climbers over it. This is quicker and easier than using box.

Small trees, singled out as specimens, can look very attractive when used in a confined space. Even this ornamental maple, if tub-grown as here, can be moved if this container garden is re-organised.

CHOOSING YOUR PLANTS

Finding the right plant for the right situation can be tricky, especially when you are faced with a huge array at a garden centre. In this chapter you will find some guide-lines to help you in your choice. But do not be afraid to experiment: some of the most unlikely seeming plants can turn out to be the most impact-making and successful.

Permanent plants for window-boxes

Aubrieta Low-growing, hardy evergreens that prefer a limy soil but are easy to grow. The flowers, which appear from March to June, are usually in the pink-purple colour range. *A. Aurea* has leaves tinged with gold.

Buxus sempervirens (box) makes a good evergreen mini-hedge or can be trained into topiary. It will take shade and will grow to a maximum of 600 mm (24 in).
B. sempervirens 'Aurea' is a golden version of the plant which grows slightly larger.

Convallaria (lily-of-the-valley) Plants that like partial shade; they spread quickly and will need thinning out from time to time. The waxy, white, bell-like flowers appear in April and May, or earlier in a warm, sheltered spot.

Cryptomeria japonica 'Elegans Compacta' is a miniature form of Japanese cedar with blue-green leaves that turn red-bronze in winter. It rarely reaches more than about 750 mm (30 in) high and wide.

Erica carnea (syn. *E. herbacea*; winter heath) is a winter-flowering plant which should bloom from December through to May; flowers white or pale pink, height not more than 300 mm (12 in).

Page 110 Begonias are among the most adaptable, good-natured plants you can choose for a small setting. Here they make a very attractive pattern in matching baskets and border.

Hebe (veronica) species also make useful evergreen mini-bushes bearing small white flowers in summer. *H.* 'Autumn glory' has purplish green leaves; *H.* 'Pagei' has light green leaves and is the smallest version, reaching about 300 mm (12 in).

Hedera (ivy) can be used as an evergreen trailer or climber, or as ground cover in boxes and hanging baskets.

Juniperus communis 'Compressa' is a dwarf juniper that has pleasant grey-green foliage and grows about 750 mm (30 in) high

Lavandula compacta nana A short, bushy version of lavender growing little more than 150 mm (6 in) high; useful for box edgings.

Lysimachia nummularia (creeping jenny) A useful ground-cover plant if you are planning a window box in reds and oranges; it bears bright-yellow, cup-shaped flowers in June and July.

Rosa. Miniature roses come in all the colours that large-size roses are found in and will grow about 450 mm (18 in) high. They need a rich soil and some sun.

Saxifraga × urbium (London pride) The most familiar member of the vast saxifrage family, it prefers shade and produces masses of small pink flowers in early summer.

Senecio compactus, a small evergreen shrub with silver grey foliage, may need clipping; it will reach up to 900 mm (36 in).

Vinca minor (lesser periwinkle) is a useful evergreen ground-cover plant for boxes and hanging baskets. It has bright blue flowers in summer and will spread or trail about 450 mm (18 in).

A permanently planted, easy to manage window-box or trough can still provide you with plenty of colour. Here, from left to right, are lesser periwinkle (*Vinca minor*), a useful trailer; *Hebe* 'Pagei', which flowers in early summer; miniature roses; aubrieta; heath *Erica carnea*, another trailer; a miniature form of common juniper, *Juniperus communis* 'Compressa', fronted by another miniature rose; a compact lavender, *Lavandula* 'Hidcote'; a variegated form of common ivy (*Hedera helix*); and London pride (*Saxifraga × urbium*).

Bedding plants for window-boxes and hanging baskets

Colour is the keynote when you are making your selection of display plants for window-boxes and hanging baskets. Never be afraid to experiment: daring combinations like hot red with oranges and yellows can be quite spectacular in a small setting. Switch your schemes round from one year to the next to vary the centres of colour.

Ageratum houstonianum A Michaelmas-daisy-like flower from Mexico. 'Blue Chip' is a long-flowering variety, as is 'Fairy Pink'.

Alyssum Good standbys available in almost all colours of the rainbow now. Cut back well after flowering to keep them in shape.

Antirrhinum (snapdragon). Choose the dwarf bedding varieties which grow about 225 mm (9 in) tall, plant them out in May, and they should flower from June through to late September. If you are growing from seed, sow in February or March.

Begonia semperflorens is a fibrous-rooted bedding begonia which comes in many colours from white through yellow to deep reds and pinks, with leaves that are green or bronze. Plant out in May. The flowers, which bloom all summer until the first frosts, are tiny compared with those of the tuberous begonias, whose blooms resemble those of petunias. Height 150–200 mm (6–8 in).

Calceolaria (slipper flower). Often grown as indoor plants, calceolarias have distinctive spotted, pouch-shaped flowers in reds and yellows. They can be planted out after the last frosts and will go on through the summer. They grow 300–400 mm (12–16 in) high and need plenty of sunlight.

Callistephus chinensis (Chinese aster). The many cultivars of this species have flowers that vary from those looking like a daisy to complicated chrysanthemum-like blooms. Flowers come in pinks, blues, and white and bloom from July to autumn. Plants grow 225–300 mm (9–12 in) high. Bed out in May.

Campanula isophylla. A relative of the Canterbury bell, this plant can be grown only in a window-box in a sheltered position, but it rewards you with heart-shaped leaves and starry, bell-like flowers. A true dwarf plant, it grows only 150–225 mm (6–9 in) high.

Celosia argentea (cockscomb). The dwarf

varieties of this plant – look for 'Golden Feather', 'Fiery Feather', 'Lilliput Mixed', or 'Jewel Box' – have plume-like flowers in reds and yellows and grow 300–400 mm (12–16 in) high. Plant them out in June and they will flower until September.

Centaurea (cornflower) comes in other shades than cornflower blue – deep scarlet, for instance. Cornflowers are best grown in situ from seed sown in March or bedded out in May. Choose *C. imperialis* for the shortest plants, growing to about 450 mm (18 in) high. Cornflowers should blossom all summer through, but you need to give them plenty of sun.

Cheiranthus × *allionii* (Siberian wallflower). Buy as a bedding plant or sow the seed in autumn to bloom the following summer. This dwarf species will grow up to 400 mm (16 in) high. Varieties have yellow, orange, and red flowers which appear in late spring and early summer.

Chrysanthemum frutescens is a bushy perennial which produces generous quantities of flowers through the summer – white daisies with yellow centres. Plant it out in May and keep it going indoors or under shelter in the winter. An ideal plant to train as a flowering standard, too. It needs plenty of sunshine.

Cineraria (strictly *Senecio* species) are very popular bedding plants for window-boxes that can also be grown indoors. They produce masses of close-packed flowers in the spring. *Senecio cruentus* (syn. *Cineraria cruenta*) 'Gem Mixed' is a good variety. Cinerarias are half-hardy and they are usually bought as pot plants and put outside once the weather is warmer.

Cobaea scandens (cathedral bell). A climber/trailer with bell-like purple flowers that bloom freely from May to October, and dark green leaves.

Coleus (flame nettles) are bushy plants, often grown indoors, which are valued mainly for their multi-coloured leaves and winter flowers. They grow about 450 mm (18 in) high and add foliage colour to hanging baskets and boxes, but look rather 'hot'. They can be taken indoors to decorate the house in winter. Plant out of doors in June.

Cucurbita pepo ovifera. Attractive ornamental gourds to cut and keep for winter decoration indoors; the bush types need less space than trailing types.

Fuchsia 'Falling Stars', Begonia semperflorens, and trailing blue lobelia go well together in a hanging basket.

Calceolarias, often grown as indoor plants, combine with morning glory (Ipomoea) and night-scented stock (Matthiola bicornis).

Cup-and-saucer plant (Cobaea scandens), China aster (Callistephus), and Mesembryanthemum

Dianthus barbatus (sweet william). Plant out in May; the plant blooms in June and July. If you remove the flower stems immediately after flowering, the plants should bloom again the following year.

Eccremocarpus scaber (Chilean glory flower). A climber/trailer that bears rich, tubular, orange-red flowers from June to October.

Fuchsia hybrids are ideal plants for plenty of show with their purple and pink flowers. They appreciate sunlight and plenty of water or they wilt. Dead-head the flowers frequently to get a succession of blooms. Plant out in June, bring indoors if you want them to over-winter. They grow up to 1 m ($3\frac{1}{4}$ ft) high, and can be trained as standards.

Gazania rigens (syn. *G. splendens*; treasure flower) is a low-growing, attractive, bushy plant with bright orange, pink, or scarlet daisy-like flowers with attractive markings in the centre. It grows 300–400 mm (12–16 in) high and must have bright sunlight. Plant it out in June.

Heliotropium × hybridum (heliotrope or cherry pie). Small fragrant flowers in blues through to dark violet, which bloom from May through to October. It grows 300–450 mm (12–18 in) high and can be trained as a standard. It can be taken indoors to grow on for another year.

Impatiens (busy lizzie) are good plants for hanging baskets, boxes and small tubs. *I. balsamina* (balsam) can be grown outdoors in summer, but bring it in if there is danger of frost. 'Camellia Flowered Mixed' and 'Tom Thumb Mixed' both have double flowers. 'Scarlet Baby' is a good bedding plant. They grow up to 60 cm (24 in) high and flower from April to October.

Ipomoea (morning glory) are climbers or trailers with pretty bell-like flowers in blue and white. They must have full sun and in a rich soil will make 3 m (10 ft) of growth.

Lathyrus odoratus (sweet pea) is a trailer or climber with a huge variety of flower colours from deep burgundy to white. Choose 'Snoopea' if you want a bushy, non-trailing variety. Set the plants out in May.

Lobelia. Make sure you buy a trailing variety. Flowers are now available in reds and white as well as Oxford and Cambridge blues. Plant out in May and they will flower in June/July through to September.

Matthiola (stock) are cottage flowers that thrive in boxes and baskets. *M. bicornis* is the night-scented stock, which bears perfumed lavender flowers in June and July. Other varieties come in pinks, blues, and white. The group known as Brompton stocks, if planted out in March, will bloom through to May; plant out the others in May for summer blooms.

Maurandia scandens. Another trailer with attractive tubular flowers in deep violet-purple.

Mesembryanthemum criniflorum (syn. *Dirotheanthus bellediformis*; Livingstone daisy). Plant this in June and you will have rich pink and orange flowers from July to September. This tiny succulent plant seldom grows more than 150 mm (6 in) high. It likes plenty of sun.

Nemesia strumosa makes compact plants with large flowers in a variety of colours: 'Suttons Mixed' is in red orange tones; 'Blue Gem' has blue flowers. Plant in full sunlight in May; they will flower through midsummer.

Nicotiana (tobacco plant) are plants grown as much for their head fragrance as for their looks. Flowers come in white, sharp yellow-green, and reds; the plants tend to sprawl to 600 mm (24 in). Plant them in May and they will bloom from July to September.

Pelargonium (geranium) is a great window-box and hanging-basket standby. Choose the zonal varieties for height and the ivy-leafed varieties for climbers or trailers. Look out for scented-leaved varieties, too; their flowers are unremarkable, but the fine-toothed leaves are fragrant and attractive. Plant geraniums out in May and they will flower through until October. Bring them indoors to overwinter, or take cuttings for the following year. Geraniums appreciate sunlight, but will thrive in semi-shade.

Petunia × hybrida is one of the showiest window-box plants with white, pink, red, or blue flowers. It can be had in standard, dwarf, or trailing varieties and is very good for hanging baskets as well as for boxes. Plant out in May and it will bloom to September, growing about 300 mm (12 in) high.

Primula (polyanthus). Planted out in March, these useful hybrid versions of the primrose (often listed as *Primula vulgaris elatior*) will bloom throughout the latter part of spring

Busy lizzie (*Impatiens*) is mixed here with pink ivy-leaved geraniums (*Pelargonium*) and the brush-like ageratum.

Pink and mauve stocks (*Matthiola*) go well with annual *Chrysanthemum frutescens* and trailer *Maurandia*, an evergreen.

Cornflower (*Centaurea cyanus*) with mother-of-thousands (*Saxifraga stolonifera*) and *Alyssum*.

and can be left as permanent occupants of the box, provided that they are divided from time to time after flowering.

Salvia species are colourful plants with bright red spike-like flowers that are good for formal boxes. Plant them out in May when they will grow to about 300 mm (12 in) high and bloom until autumn.

Saxifraga stolonifera (syn. *S. sarmentosa*; mother of thousands), often grown as a houseplant, can also be grown out of doors, although it is not very hardy and is best

brought indoors for the winter. It is grown for its colourful leaves – green tinged with pink and silver with plantlets on runners. Plant rosettes in May or June. A useful plant for colourful ground cover in a box.

Tagetes (marigold). Choose the French marigold (*T. patula*) if you want a low-growing plant; the African variety (*T. erecta*) reaches 450 mm (18 in) or more. Delicately scented, the African marigold has pompon blooms in pale yellows through to red; the French marigold has single or double flowers in the same colours. Both

species should bloom from the time they are planted out in May through to the first frosts. But they must have plenty of sunlight.

Verbena peruviana. A low-growing plant that bears scarlet spikes of star-like flowers; it needs shelter in the winter.

Viola tricolor (heartsease) is a pretty low-grower, seldom reaching more than 225 mm (9 in) in height, which comes in a wide variety of colours; it can be planted in October to flower the following March. If you put it out in May it will bloom in

midsummer. *V. × wittrockiana* (garden pansy). Choose cultivars such as 'Celestial Queen' and 'Ice King', which bloom in the late autumn and winter months.

Zinnia elegans is very like a chrysanthemum to look at; the compact cultivar 'Lilliput', which grows 250 mm (10 in) high, is the best for boxes and baskets. But if you want a particularly small plant, choose 'Thumbelina', which barely reaches 150 mm (6 in). Both have multicoloured flowers. Plant them out in May and they will bloom until September, but put them in full sun.

Summer colour, from left: *Campanula isophylla* (foreground), a dwarf version of the bellflower; in the background, two petunias, *P.* 'Peach Satin' and *P.* 'Apple Blossom'. Next, in the foreground, 'L'Elegante', a form of the ivy-leaved geranium (*Pelargonium peltatum*); then an appealing small version of heartsease (*Viola tricolor*), with sweet william (*Dianthus*) in the background; and finally a blue lobelia backed by antirrhinums.

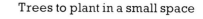

Trees to plant in a small space

Although almost every garden will benefit from the extra dimension of height given by trees, take care when choosing trees for a small space, or you could end up with problems in years to come if they outgrow their welcome. Within the most popular groups there are plenty of smaller species or dwarf forms to choose from.

Acer griseum. A marvellous small Chinese maple for late summer colour, when the leaves turn scarlet and the trunk and branches have a flaky, orange-brown bark to match. *A. palmatum* (Japanese maple) is a small tree with attractive pink 'keys' (fruits) in the autumn rather like those of the sycamore. A good ornamental tree, its many cultivars are outstanding for autumn colour.

Amelanchier canadensis (shadbush). A hardy little tree that produces a mass of

white flowers in late spring, and with leaves that turn yellow-red in autumn. Its edible black berries ripen in June.

Betula pendula 'Tristis' (weeping silver birch). A pretty tree for a small space as long as its roots are reasonably well confined.

Chamaecyparis lawsoniana 'Elwoodii' and 'Minima glauca' are two varieties of the Lawson cypress that are good for tubs.

Cotoneaster include many species and varieties that grow 2.6 m (8 ft) or less high; most bear attractive berries.

Cytisus (broom), of which many species are suitable as wall shrubs or as ground cover.

Davidia involucrata vilmoriniana (pocket-handkerchief tree). An unusual small tree with creamy bracts on it, not unlike those on a poinsettia, which are often mistaken for flowers.

Juniperus communis 'Compressa' and 'Aurea' (two varieties of common juniper that are good for tubs).

Laburnum alpinum (Scotch laburnum). With showers of golden flowers in late spring or early summer and unusual 'corkscrew' branches, this makes an attractive tree for a garden corner.

Magnolia × *soulangiana*.

Malus sargentii (crab apple) is one of the smallest crab apples, with small berry-like fruits.

Pinus mugo (mountain pine). A small pine tree with needles borne in clusters.

Some trees suitable for planting in a small space. Left to right: *Betula pendula*, the weeping form of the silver birch; *Juniperus compressa* 'Depressa Aurea', a low-growing juniper; a golden broom (*Cytisus*); *Rhododendron* 'Glory of Littleworth'; a flowering cherry (*Prunus*); and a dwarf mountain pine (*Pinus mugo*).

P.m. pumilio is a dwarf version, growing no higher than a man; there are also prostrate forms.

Prunus (flowering cherry).

Rhododendron. Many forms, some of which are listed as trees and others as shrubs, grow no more than 3–4.5 m (10–15 ft) high.

Sophora japonica (Japanese pagoda tree). An attractive slow-growing tree with long, slim leaves and small white flowers which appear in September.

Sorbus scopulina 'Decora Nana' is a slow-growing, columnar tree; bright red fruits.

Tsuga canadensis 'Pendula' (weeping eastern hemlock) is a bush growing to 1.8 m (6 ft) high and 3 m (10 ft) wide.

Trees and shrubs for autumn or winter colour

The most attractive town gardens have some colour in them all the year round. For basic background colour you can rely on evergreen shrubs and trees throughout the year. Autumn brings the fiery tints of leaves on the turn. In winter plenty of attractive plants come into bloom, while many trees and shrubs have colourful stems.

Acer (maple) offers a variety of autumn colour. *A. griseum* (paperbark maple), will reward you with colourful bark and deep scarlet leaves in the autumn, but needs plenty of sun and the space of a small garden or courtyard. *A. palmatum* 'Senkaki' (coral-barked Japanese maple), on the other hand, will not grow more than 3.6 m (12 ft) high and has coral red bark and yellow leaves in the autumn.

Callicarpa bodinieri giraldii is a shrub that grows a maximum of 2 m (6½ ft) high. In autumn it has violet berries and its narrow leaves turn yellow and red. It has a bonus of lilac flowers that appear in July, making it a good all-rounder to plant in a small space.

Chamaecyparis lawsoniana 'Lutea' is an autumnal variety of Lawson cypress that forms a column about 2 m (6½ ft) high and has golden-yellow foliage.

Chimonanthus praecox (winter sweet) is a winter stalwart which produces pale yellow flowers at the beginning of the year. It is a shrub that is best grown against a wall, reaching about 3 m (10 ft) high.

Cornus alba 'Sibirica' (Westonbirt red-barked dogwood). Plant this variety of dogwood if you want red leaves in autumn and red stems in winter. *C. stolonifera* 'Flaviramea' has yellow stems in winter. Both grow to about 1.5 m (5 ft).

Daphne mezereum (Mezereon). An attractive shrub growing about 1.2 m (4 ft) high which has scented pink flowers in late winter and scarlet berries in early summer. *Warning*: the berries are highly poisonous, so this plant should not be grown if young children frequent your garden.

Erica carnea (winter heath) is good for a window-box or tub as well as a garden bed. It flowers in the winter and grows only about 300 mm (12 in) high.

Fatsia japonica (false castor-oil plant) is ideal if you want a tropical look to a terrace, this evergreen shrub, which grows up to 2 m (6½ ft) tall unless checked, has creamy white flowers throughout the winter months.

Garrya elliptica (silk-tassel bush) goes well against a wall. It has long, pale green catkins in January and February. Treated as a climber it will grow to 2.4 m (8 ft).

Hamamelis mollis (Chinese witch hazel) is a shrub with golden leaves in autumn and yellow flowers tinged with red in January. It grows up to 2.1 m (7 ft) high.

Ilex aquifolium (holly) has bright red berries for Christmas cheer; it can be clipped into classic shapes for a tub.

Kerria japonica 'Pleniflora' (Jew's mallow) has bright green stems that look good against a wall in winter. It produces double yellow flowers in late spring and grows 2 m (6½ ft) high.

Mahonia bealii. This evergreen shrub bears trailing, lemon-yellow flowers which appear about Christmas time and stay until February.

Malus 'Red Sentinel'. A small crab-apple tree, bearing clusters of bright scarlet fruits that stay on the tree throughout the winter and well into spring.

Parrotia persica. This tree, which grows 4.5 m (15 ft) or less, has magnificent autumn foliage; in adult trees the bark flakes to make an attractive pattern in the winter.

Pernettya mucronata. A hardy shrub of the heather family which has red stems and produces clusters of attractive pink fruits which last through the winter. To ensure fruiting, grow several of these plants together.

Prunus subhirtella 'Autumnalis' (autumn cherry). This tree produces white flowers from November through to March.

Rubus cockburnianus. A member of the raspberry-blackberry family, this ornamental deciduous shrub is grown for its unusual straight-standing white stems.

Skimmia japonica. An attractive shrub with leathery green leaves and white, sweet-smelling flowers; its bright red berries stay on the plant all through the winter.

Viburnum farreri (syn. *V. fragrans*). A useful deciduous shrub which has rose-tinged white flowers on its bare branches from December through to February.

Some trees and shrubs that go well in pots and give autumn and winter colour. Left to right: *Erica carnea*, the heather that can cope with less-acid soils; *Fatsia japonica*, the false castor-oil plant; *Thuja orientalis* 'Aurea Nana'; *Skimmia japonica*; a maple (*Acer*); *Mahonia bealii*, which bears lemon-yellow flowers in mid-winter; and, in the foreground, winter sweet (*Chimonanthus praecox*).

Some plants for a well-stocked small pond. Left to right: water soldier (*Stratiotes aloides*); *Iris pseudacorus* 'Variegata'; two water lilies, *Nymphaea laydekeri* 'Lilacea' and *N. pygmaea* 'Helvola', with yellow flowers. In the background are water starwort (*Callitriche stagnalis*), the water violet (*Hottonia palustris*), and *Orontium aquaticum*, with *Trapa natans* in the front of them and, at the end, *Iris laevigata* 'Oxford Blue', which grows best in just a few inches of water.

Plants for mini-ponds and pools

Water can provide a delightful centre of interest in a small garden, and even a balcony can be fitted out with its own mini-pond or pool. Your pond can be anything from a glass bowl to a pool complete with fountain. The larger pools should be stocked not just with aquatics but with plants around the edges to provide added impact.

Azolla caroliniana (fairy floating moss) is a floating fern that creates a carpet over the surface of a pool and helps cut down light. Its leaves have a reddish tinge and it dies down in winter.

Callitriche stagnalis (water starwort) is a useful oxygenator that keeps algae at bay. It needs planting in heavy soil at the bottom of a pool, where it spreads to form a mat.

Eichhornia crassipes (syn. *E. speciosa*; water hyacinth) produces showy spikes of purple flowers usually with blue and/or gold marks on the petals, and it floats on the surface of a

this has strange, sensitive leaves which shrink away from you when you touch them.

Nymphaea 'Aurora' (water lily) will grow in as little as 150 mm (6 in) of water. It has yellow flowers that turn to orange, and mottled purple leaves. *N. × laydekeri* 'Fulgens', with crimson flowers, will also take shallow water, and *N. × laydekeri* 'Lilacea' has pink lilac flowers and is scented. *N. pygmaea alba* has small white flowers and can be planted in 150 mm (6 in) of water; so can *N. pygmaea* 'Helvola', which has yellow flowers and mottled green leaves.

Orontium aquaticum (golden club). A pond-side version of the red-hot poker in appearance, but with yellow flowers, this is a plant that grows best at a depth of not more than 225 mm (9 in).

Stratiotes aloides (water soldier) has clusters of leaves rather like pineapple tops floating in the water, and white flowers that poke up through the surface from June

pond. It should be transferred to a bowl of wet soil indoors from September to May.

Hottonia palustris (water violet). Ideal for a lily pond, this plant will stand the cold and does not mind being shaded. It has bright green leaves tinged with red and, later, beautiful violet flowers. It develops buds in winter, then dies down until spring.

Neptunia oleracea. An unusual plant from North America with bright yellow flowers,

through to August. It will happily withstand quite cold winters.

Trapa natans (water chestnut). Unusual mottled leaves are a feature of this plant, which has small white flowers whose seeds are used for making rosaries.

Ranunculus aquatilis (water crowfoot). Easily recognisable as a member of a buttercup family by its familiar yellow flowers.

Plants for tubs and small flower beds

Accent plants which give colour just where it is wanted are a valuable asset in a small town garden, but the larger specimens need a little more room than the average window box can provide. This is where larger containers come into their own; and if you have space in the form of flower beds, many of these plants will go there too.

Acanthus (bear's breeches) are attractive foliage plants with tall spikes of flowers varying from lavender to white. They grow 600–900 mm (2–3 ft) tall and flower in midsummer.

Achillea (yarrow). The dwarf varieties of this plant are good for rockeries or containers. *A. chrysocoma* grows 100 mm (4 in) high, has woolly grey-green leaves and yellow flowers, and flowers in July. *A. clavenae* has white daisy-like blooms in early summer.

Adonis amurensis is a low-growing, attractive plant with bright yellow flowers and fern-like foliage which prefers a partially shaded situation and is good to underplant among taller plants. It produces flowers in early spring.

Aethionema pulchellum is a compact plant growing 150–225 mm (6–9 in) high with attractive dark pink flowers in May and June. Basically a rockery plant, it grows well in tubs and window-boxes.

Agapanthus (African lily) are showy specimen plants for tubs and small borders. They can also be grown in a box alongside a terrace. Choose the hardy variety *A. inapertus*, which has deep violet-blue flowers in July–August and which grows about 450 mm (18 in) high.

Agave are marvellous foliage plants, especially if you want a tropical look in a tub or a border. *A. americana* 'Marginata' (syn. 'Variegata') has narrow sword-like leaves edged with gold, *A. victoriae-reginae* forms a pompon head like a cactus. They are not completely hardy and are best brought indoors during the winter.

Ageratum are good summer bedding flowers, rather like large Michaelmas daisies, that are useful in boxes. Choose *A. houstonianum* 'Fairy Pink' or 'Blue Mink' for a good show of colour. They grow 150–300 mm (6–12 in) high and bloom through the summer until the first frosts.

Alchemilla (lady's mantle). Another handsome foliage plant that is often used for flower arrangements and which looks good in a tub. *A. mollis* has star-shaped yellow-green flowers and will self-seed itself. It grows 300–450 mm (12–18 in) high and flowers from June to September.

Allium giganteum is a decorative form of onion which makes a good feature plant in a small bed. It forms deep lilac flower heads which can be dried for decoration indoors. It grows up to 1.2 m (4 ft) high and flowers in June and July.

Alstroemeria (Peruvian lily) is another striking plant which has flowers somewhere between those of orchids and gladioli in appearance. *A. aurantiaca* grows up to 1m (3 ft) high and has flowers ranging from yellow to scarlet in midsummer.

Alyssum is a reliable carpeting plant for tubs, dry-stone walls and rockeries. *A. argenteum* has bright yellow flowers in June through to August. *A. maritimum* (strictly, *Lobularia maritima*) has white or lilac flowers and is low-growing.

Anagallis arvensis (scarlet pimpernel). A pretty, prostrate plant with small red flowers. It is an annual, but it will generally self-seed for the next year. *A. arvensis* 'Caerulea' is another form which has dark blue flowers from July through to October and grows less than 100 mm (4 in) high.

Anemone × hybrida (syn. *A. japonica*; Japanese windflower). An attractive large-flowered version of the anemone which looks rather like a dahlia. The variety 'Queen Charlotte' has attractive semi-double pink flowers.

Anthemis (chamomile). There are many forms of this plant, ranging from the carpeting (non-flowering) *Anthemis nobilis* 'Treneague' to the yellow or ox-eye chamomile (*A. tinctoria*). One of the most decorative varieties is *A. sancti-johannis*, which comes from Bulgaria, grows about 450 mm (18 in) high and has bright orange flowers.

Aquilegia (columbine). Delicate, attractive flowers to grow in a small space, where they are most appreciated. *A. longissima* has pretty yellow flowers on slender stems; *A. bertolonii* is a small Alpine version that looks, at a distance, rather like edelweiss; *A. vulgaris*, which comes in many colours, is the best-known columbine.

Armeria (thrift) are useful plants to edge a tub or go between paving stones. They produce hummocks of spiky grass-like leaves and pink flower heads from May to August. There are several different species, ranging from *A. caespitosa*, which grows only 50–75 mm (2–3 in) high, to *A. maritima* which can reach 300 mm (12 in).

Artemisia are grown for their silvery white leaves; they are useful plants to have in a mixed border, especially with colourful annual flowers. *A. stelleriana* (dusty miller) has leaves that are almost white, and yellow flowers in August and September. *A. gnaphalodes* has woolly white leaves. Both grow to about 600 mm (24 in) high.

Asperula suberosa is a small semi-trailing plant (a relative of sweet woodruff) that has a profusion of pretty pink flowers in June and July. It grows 50–75 mm (2–3 in) tall and has white, hairy leaves.

Aster is a large genus, best known for the Michaelmas daisies. Asters have flowers in purples, blues, reds, and pinks. The smallest plant is *A. alpinus*, which grows just 150 mm (6 in) high and has purple-blue flowers with orange-yellow centres in July. If you are buying a true Michaelmas daisy (such as *A. novibelgii*), pick a dwarf variety such as 'Audrey' which grows to 300 mm (12 in), 'Lady in Blue', 250 mm (10 in), or 'Professor Kippenburg', 225 mm (9 in). All flower in August and September.

Aubrieta are something colourful to depend on as ground cover in a tub or a window-box. *A. deltoidea* is one of the most attractive forms, with rose-lilac flowers that appear in late spring or early summer. *Aubrieta* appreciate a sunny position.

Begonia are a great standby for tubs, hanging baskets, and window-boxes. The fibrous-rooted *B. semperflorens* makes a good bedding plant, growing 150–225 mm (6–9 in) high. It flowers all through the summer and often well into the autumn frosts. It has small flowers in red, pink, or white, and leaves ranging from glossy green to bronze-purple. The tuberous-rooted begonias of the Pendula group make good trailers for hanging baskets, while *Begonia rex*, a plant that grows from a rhizome, is good for special display.

Bellis (daisy). Double or pompon forms flower from March to October. Look for *B. perennis* 'Monstrosa' for showy flowers and plants 150–225 mm (6–9 in) high. They are good for underplanting.

Calendula officinalis (pot marigold) is the true marigold, with its double daisy-like flowers in bright orange (though you can also get versions with creamy, apricot, even pink flowers). 'Kelmscott Giant Orange' is a good one to choose; 'Pacific Beauty' will give you a mixture of colours. Marigolds can stand the poorest soil, grow up to 600 mm (2 ft) high, and will flower through the summer to the first frosts in autumn.

Callirhoe are basically rock-garden plants; they are dwarf trailers with simple bowl-shaped, mauve-red flowers produced in mid-summer. *C. involucrata* is a good version to choose. It grows about 150 mm (6 in) high.

Callistephus chinensis (Chinese aster). Choose 'Lilliput Mixed' for a good display, with flowers ranging from white to crimson. It grows 400 mm (16 in) high, and bears a mass of flowers all summer. A good choice for small tubs.

Canna × generalis bears showy, tropical-looking flowers and makes a good specimen in tubs. Among good cultivars are 'Orange Perfection', which grows just over 600 mm (2 ft) high, and 'President', which is a little taller and has bright scarlet flowers.

Chionodoxa are good spring-flowering bulbs to go under permanent plantings in a tub. Glory-of-the-snow (*C. luciliae*) grows 150 mm (6 in) tall and has light blue flowers with white centres; *C. sardensis* reaches 100–150 mm (4–6 in), and has deeper-blue flowers.

Chrysanthemum. A huge range of very reliable flowers for tubs and boxes. Some are annuals, others are perennials. Look for the attractive alpine species. *C. alpinum* for very-small-scale planting. It has white daisy-like flowers in July and August and grows only 150 mm (6 in) tall. *C. carinatum*, a North African annual, is much taller, and has very colourful flowers from June to September.

Colchicum (autumn crocus) are useful fill-in bulbs for September through to November. *C. luteum* is the smallest, only 150–200 mm (6–8 in) tall, with pale lilac-pink blooms.

Cyclamen. The hardy outdoor forms of this popular plant are much more delicate to look at than indoor types and grow only about 100 mm (4 in) high. One of the best, *C. coum*, has pink flowers that appear from December through to March.

Dahlia. A vast variety is available, ranging from those with pompon heads to simple versions almost like huge daisies. For small areas choose the dwarf varieties of bedding dahlias; a good example is 'Early Bird', which has semi-double flowers in pink, yellow, orange, and deep red.

Dianthus (pinks and carnations). Real cottage-garden flowers, including sweet william (*D. barbatus*), which grows about 300 mm (12 in) high. *D. alpinus*, which is basically a rock garden plant, is useful if space is limited. Miniature versions of the so-called Modern pinks, which grow less than 150 mm (6 in) tall, include 'Bombadier', which has red flowers, and 'Fay', which has mauve flowers. Pinks and carnations flower in early summer, usually from the beginning of June to the middle of August.

Doronicum (leopard's bane) are daisy-like flowers which bloom early and, if dead-

A miscellany of plants for tubs and small beds. Left to right: poppies (*Papaver*), with lamb's tongue (*Stachys lanata*) and, in the foreground, thrift (*Armeria*). Then pinks (*Dianthus*); columbine (*Aquilegia*); lady's mantle (*Alchemilla mollis*); meadow crane's-bill (*Geranium pratense*); *Alyssum* and *Aubrieta*; *Godetia grandiflora*; pot marigold (*Calendula officinalis*); *Begonia rex*; dusty miller (*Artemisia stelleriana*); *Anthemis sancti-johannis*; *Geum* and *Linaria*; and, in the large urn, African lily (*Agapanthus*).

headed regularly, will often produce a second flush in the autumn. *D. columnae* (syn. *D. cordatum*) grows 200–250 mm (8–10 in) high and has single golden yellow flowers.

Erigeron (fleabane) are daisy-like plants with flowers in pinks, blues, and yellows. *E. aureus* grows 75–100 mm (3–4 in) high and bears yellow flowers about 25 mm (1 in) across in June and July.

Eschscholzia californica (Californian poppy) grows about 300 mm (12 in) tall and produces masses of orange or yellow flowers from early summer to October. If you want a dwarf species, one of the most attractive is *E. caespitosa*, which is less than 150 mm (6 in) high.

Geranium (crane's-bill) are the true geraniums, which make good plants for a tub. They have pretty pink or blue flowers and lacy leaves. *G. dalmaticum* is an almost alpine species that grows 150 mm (6 in) high and makes a broad cushion of light pink flowers from June to early September.

Geum (avens). More summer colour. These plants are good in display beds or, in the case of alpine varieties, in small window-boxes and hanging baskets. *G. montanum* and *G. reptans* are excellent dwarf versions, their yellow flowers followed by interesting silvery seed heads. They grow about 225 mm (9 in) high and flower in June, July, and August.

Godetia are hardy annuals with double or single flowers in mid-summer. *G. grandiflora* is one of the most attractive, with rose-purple blooms; its cultivar 'Azalea-flowered Mixed' has frilled petals. Both grow about 300 mm (12 in) high.

Hypericum (St John's wort) are useful yellow flowers for a permanent flower bed. Rose-of-sharon (*H. calycinum*) is the most commonly planted variety, but *H. patulum* 'Hidcote' is a much more attractive plant if you have the space for it – it reaches a height of 900 mm (3 ft) or more. St John's worts also give you berries and coloured foliage in the autumn.

Iberis (candytuft) are good plants for town gardens since they stand up well to atmospheric pollution. *I. amara* has pink-carmine flowers, grows 400 mm (16 in) high, and flowers in early summer.

Limonium (statice, or sea lavender). Ideal

for everlasting flowers when it has done its duty in summer, this attractive Mediterranean annual comes in many different colours. *L. sinuatum* and its cultivars are best if you want dried flowers for winter.

Linaria alpina (toadflax) makes a pretty plant to put among paving stones. It grows 75–150 mm (3–6 in) high and has purple bell-like flowers in June, July, and August.

Moluccella laevis (bells of Ireland) is an unusual plant with curious green flowers that make an interesting effect if put in a tub. It grows up to 600 mm (2 ft) tall, and flowers in midsummer. It looks good if mixed with white flowers, and the flower heads can be dried for winter decoration.

Nemesia strumosa is a useful plant for a mixed display, flowering from June to August. Choose the cultivar 'Carnival Mixed', which is a dwarf version that grows 225 mm (9 in) high.

Papaver (poppy) are excellent in small gardens, especially when mixed with plants with silvery foliage. If you are worried about height – most of them reach 450–600 mm (18–24 in) – choose the alpine poppy (*P. alpinum*), which is available with flowers of white, yellow, red, and orange. The Iceland poppy (*P. nudicaule*) has flowers with petals like tissue paper and is particularly attractive.

Phlox drummondii is an annual that, when used as a bedding plant, gives you good value for money, with flowers of pink, purple, lavender, red, and white. It grows about 400 mm (16 in) high and flowers from July to September.

Salvia splendens. A good standby for a splash of colour. Its cultivar 'Blaze of Fire' has particularly brilliant flowers of bright scarlet and grows about 300 mm (1 ft) high.

Stachys lanata (lamb's tongue) is grown for its distinctive woolly foliage, which makes a good foil to colourful bedding plants. But it has flowers as well – spikes of purple blooms open in midsummer. It grows about 300 mm (12 in) high.

Veronica (speedwell). A useful group of ground-cover plants ranging from *V. cinerea*, with pink flowers, which reaches a height of 100 mm (4 in), to the bright-blue-flowered *V. filiformis*, which is only 25 mm (1 in) or so high but may spread 1.2 m (4 ft).

Shrubs and climbers to plant against 'cold' walls

It comes as a pleasant surprise to many people that cold, inhospitable north-facing walls can be easily clothed in colour and made to look attractive. Take your pick from these useful climbers and free-standing shrubs. Some of them provide delightful flowers, others bear colourful berries; a few of them come up trumps when they are needed most, in winter.

Akebia quinata (scented)

Berberis × stenophylla (barberry)

Chaenomeles (Japanese quince; japonica)

Choisya ternata (Mexican orange)

Daphne odora

Elaeagnus pungens 'Aurea Maculata'

Eriobotrya japonica (loquat)

Eucryphia cordifolia

Euonymus fortunei (spindle)

Fothergilla gardenii

Garrya elliptica

Hedera colchica (Persian ivy)

Hydrangea anomala; *H. petiolaris* (Japanese climbing hydrangea)

Ilex (holly)

Jasminum nudiflorum (winter-flowering jasmine)

Kerria japonica 'Pleniflora' (bachelor's buttons)

Lonicera × brownii (scarlet-trumpet honeysuckle)

Mahonia japonica

Parthenocissus tricuspidata 'Veitchii' (Boston ivy)

Polygonum baldschuanicum (Russian vine)

Prunus cerasus 'Morello' (acid cherry)

Pyracantha (firethorn)

Rose 'Gloire de Dijon' (buff-orange climber)

Viburnum grandiflorum

Some good shrubs for a cold wall. Left to right: Persian ivy (*Hedera colchica*); *Garrya elliptica* (with catkins); Mexican orange (*Choisya ternata*); jew's mallow (*Kerria japonica*); spindle tree (*Euonymus fortunei* 'Silver Queen'); *Akebia quinata*; *Viburnum grandiflorum*; and *Daphne odora*.

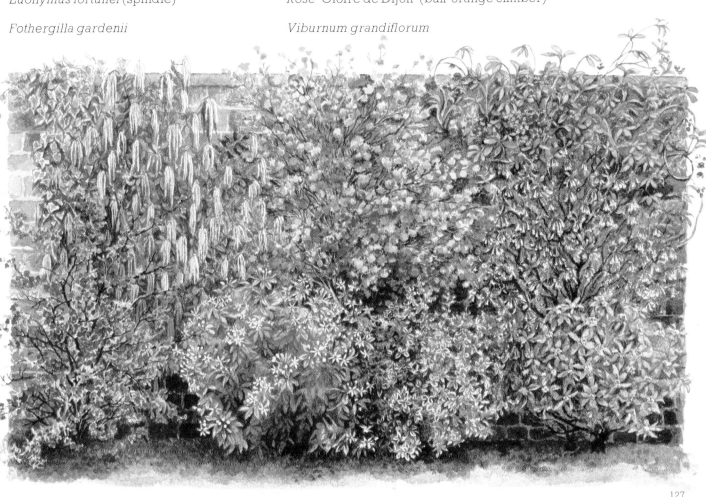

Index

Acknowledgements

A-Z Botanical Collection Ltd 48; Pat Brindley 85; Bruce Coleman Ltd (Eric Crichton) 40, 45, 49, 61, 74, 78, 80–1, (R. Tidman) 88–9, (Peter Wilby) 84; Jerry Harpur 69, 73, 107, (John Brookes) 6; Palma Studio 13, 16–17, 18–19, 20–1, 26–7, 58–9, 60, 66–7, 68, 70–1, 79, 82–3, 86–7, 109, 110; Harry Smith Horticultural Photographic Collection 12, 24, 42–3, 44, 104–5; Jessica Strang 8, 9, 29, 32–3, 34, 37, 38, 39, 50, 52, 54, 55, 58, left, 64, 65, 72, 76–7, 90, 96, 98–9, 102, 103, 106; Michael Warren 47; Elizabeth Whiting and Associates 28, 30-1, 35, 62–3, 93. Garden design, 107: Valery Stevenson Special Photography: **John Barlow** 15, 22, 100–1; **Pamla Toler** 10–11, 51, 56–7, 94–5; **Peter Rauter** 1, 2–3, 4–5. Drawings: **Gill Tomblin** 112–27. Styling: **Sonya Fancett**
We wish to thank the following for supplying plants and other materials: Jack Drumstalk, Sydney Street, London, SW3; World's End Nurseries, Kings Road, London, SW3; House of Marno, Fulham Road, London, SW6

PDO 83-1202